KILLER POKER ONLINE

D0167678

BOOKS BY JOHN VORHAUS

The Comic Toolbox: How to Be Funny Even If You're Not

Creativity Rules! A Writer's Workbook

*The Pro Poker Playbook: 223 Ways to Win More Money
Playing Poker*

Killer Poker: Strategy and Tactics for Winning Poker Play

KILLER POKER ONLINE

Crushing the Internet Game

John Vorhaus

LYLE STUART
Kensington Publishing Corp.
www.kensingtonbooks.com

LYLE STUART BOOKS are published by

Kensington Publishing Corp.
850 Third Avenue
New York, NY 10022

Copyright © 2003 John Vorhaus

All rights reserved. No part of this book may be reproduced in any form or by any means without the prior written consent of the publisher, excepting brief quotes used in reviews.

All Kensington titles, imprints, and distributed lines are available at special quantity discounts for bulk purchases for sales promotions, premiums, fund-raising, educational, or institutional use. Special book excerpts or customized printings can also be created to fit specific needs. For details, write or phone the office of the Kensington special sales manager: Kensington Publishing Corp., 850 Third Avenue, New York, NY 10022, attn: Special Sales Department, phone 1-800-221-2647.

Lyle Stuart is a trademark of Kensington Publishing Corp.

First printing: July 2003

10   9   8   7

Printed in the United States of America

ISBN 0-8184-0631-3

Dedicated to the miles of white line
we now no longer need face.

Contents

Introduction

This ain't no party,
this ain't no disco,
this ain't no fooling around.
—The Talking Heads, "Life During Wartime"

The goal of this book is to make online poker a pleasurable and profitable experience for you. That's the goal, and I'm confident that together we can achieve it. All we have to do is work hard and pay attention to some basic facts and strategies. But before we start, I want to put forth the startling idea that, hey, maybe Internet poker's not such a hot idea in the first place.

You probably think I'm wrong, flat wrong, and I wouldn't be a bit surprised. After all, you have just bought (or are browsing) a book called *Killer Poker Online: Crushing the Internet Game*. You're probably here because you, well, want to crush the Internet game. And don't worry: I'll do everything in my power to get you your money's worth—which is to say your *opponents'* money's worth—out of this book. But, look, the fact that you're here means you have a predisposition toward online poker. You approve of it. You're enthusiastic about it. Or, at minimum, you're interested in it, and you want to find out more. That's fine. You're entitled to be into what you're into. But online poker is so filled with potholes and pitfalls that I'd be remiss if I didn't temper your interest or your enthusiasm with a healthy dose of wariness, and encourage you, above all, to go slow.

Because one thing about online poker is that it's *not* slow. As you already know, or soon will know once you jump online, the pace of play there is highly accelerated, and that accelerated pace has the effect of magnifying a player's mistakes. If you weren't a terrific player to begin with . . . sigh . . . Internet poker could eat your shorts in dismayingly short order.

I'd hate to see that happen to you.

So let me ask you a question: Why do you want to play online in the first place? For fun? Money? Challenge? To kill boredom? Make friends around the world? Or is online play your only option? If you know anything about the *Killer Poker* approach to poker, then you know that in my universe the first rule is honesty; if you can't be honest with yourself about why you do what you do, you have no hope of being a winning poker player, online or anywhere. So I'll ask you again: *Why do you want to play online?*

Please write your answer here, or in the space provided at the back of the book. (If you know anything about the *Killer Poker* approach to poker, you know I'm a huge fan of writing stuff down, for the sake of honesty and clarity both.)

_____

_____

Are you here just for fun? If so, then online poker may very well meet your needs. It is, in some sense, like a home game that's always there and never ends—except that the game takes place in homes and offices and Internet cafés all around the world. If you want to play poker for fun, this book will serve you; you'll learn how to maximize your fun while minimizing your risk.

Are you here to make money? Well, then, you're on much shakier ground. Being a consistent winner playing poker online will require everything this book has to offer, plus all of your skill, stamina, effort, and dedication. You *can* be a winning player online, but it's by no means easy, and it doesn't happen by magic. Let me be clear on this point: You're only marginally more likely to become rich by playing Internet poker than by sending some online scam artist the number of your bank account.

Do you play poker for challenge? You'll find plenty of challenge in online poker, just as you would in any serious poker game anywhere. Testing yourself against competition from around the world, you may very well find that the quality of your own play goes up. It had better go up, or you'll soon find yourself swamped by the competition. Online poker, as you will see, is a grim Darwinian schoolyard, where you either improve or die—get skilled or get broke. So if competition is your goal, be prepared to give it your all. After all, there are plenty of people out there willing to devote the time, energy, and concentration it takes to be successful. If you're not willing to devote that same time, energy, and concentration, the least you can do is not let them be successful at your expense.

Is boredom your bugbear? Do you find yourself playing your umpteen millionth game of solitaire or Tetris and wishing there were a better buzz to meet your compurecreational needs? If that's what brings you to Internet poker, then tread very cautiously, because this ain't solitaire and it sure as spit ain't Tetris. The minute you put real money into play, the stakes go up of course—but, paradoxically, the boredom doesn't necessarily disappear. As you will discover, attention deficit disorder is one of the online player's greatest foes. Strange to say, you could actually end up being *more* bored, not *less* bored, when you're playing poker online. At least with Tetris, it's always your turn.

Want to make friends around the world? Well, there is a chat function on almost all online poker sites, which gives you the option of saying, *Hi, hello, nice hand, how could you play that swill?* and so on, but as for making Internet friends, and planning a rendezvous in Vegas, *nah,* it ain't gonna happen. Those people out there, they want to take your money. You'd better want to take theirs, too, or you won't be around for long.

No alternative? Some people play poker online because, sadly for them, it's the only game in town. They live in cities, states, or countries where casinos and cardrooms do not exist or are not legal. If you're in that category then you have a special quandary, because you like poker, love poker, want to play poker, and, generally speaking, you cannot. "Thank God for the Internet," you find yourself saying. At last you have an option. But it is an option fraught with at least as many problems as opportunities.

Some people think of online poker as some kind of gold rush waiting to be exploited. They plan to get rich quick, in the privacy of their own homes, by preying on hapless masses with short skill sets and long lines of credit. If that's how you view online poker, I promise that you will be disappointed. I mean think about it: Who ever gets rich in a gold rush? The miners? Nope. It's the grocers and the bankers and the surveyors, assayers and purveyors of whiskey and sin. If you really want to get rich, that's the business to be in. But getting rich, I hazard to guess, is of secondary, or even tertiary importance to you. After all, no matter why we think we want to play poker on the Internet, one common denominator binds us all: *We want to play poker.* If we can make some money at it, great. But mostly we just want to play.

The average poker player is no more likely to become a professional, full-time poker player online than he is to become a professional, full-time poker player in cardrooms or casinos. It's possible, sure. Just not likely. This we know. This we know going in. Still, that's not the end of the world. Most people don't expect to make a living from their poker. They just want their hobby to pay for itself, and that is an altogether reasonable goal. If you just keep your psychic and financial investments reasonable, then Internet poker can be a fun and fruitful part of your life. It's my job to help you make it so.

Acknowledgments

"If I have seen further," said Sir Isaac Newton, "it is by standing upon the shoulders of giants." In writing this book, I have taken note of the opinions, observations, experiences, and resources available to me (and to anyone) on the Internet, particularly the discussion group rec.gambling.poker. Though I rarely post, I often lurk, and the discourse there on the subject of Internet poker is always most insightful—if often most heated. So I would like to thank all those posters, named and unnamed, who have shaped my thoughts on the subject of online poker. I would also like to thank all of the "named names" who allowed me to quote them here. Thanks also to Kathryn Duffy for "practice makes progress."

I want to thank my wife, Maxx Duffy, for her staunch immunity to my stress during the fevered weeks and months of this book's genesis; also my agent and indispensable voice of reason, Greg Dinkin; and finally Evan Viola, for overt and covert contributions.

KILLER POKER ONLINE

1

♣ ♠ ♦ ♥

TRUE FACTS OF ONLINE POKER

First fact: Online poker is not the same as online gambling. If you put your money into play at www.joyofslots.com or www.casinofishie.com or any other online gambling site I might make up, one thing is for sure: you will not win. Not in the long run. It's just not possible, for the same reason that you can't beat Las Vegas: If you could beat Vegas, Vegas wouldn't be there. When you play casino games— slots, craps, roulette—you're playing against the house, and you're playing against the immutable house edge. While you might beat that edge in the short run, you will eventually go broke. This is true whether you're in Las Vegas or Atlantic City or the cozy computer nook of your very own home. Playing against the house is a guaranteed losing proposition.

But when you play poker, either in the real world or in cyberspace, you're not playing against the house. You're playing against other players. Maybe good ones. Maybe dreadful. The odds, as such, don't favor them or favor you. In the long run, everyone gets their fair share of good cards and bleak cards. The difference is what you do with the cards you get, and that difference is called *skill*. Poker skill.

The house is just the host, which means that with Internet poker, unlike Internet gambling, you do have a chance to win.

When I speak of poker skill, I assume you already have plenty. I assume that your knowledge of poker goes well beyond what-beats-what, and into a fairly sophisticated understanding of the poker games commonly played on the Internet: seven-card stud, Omaha, and, especially, Texas hold'em. If I'm wrong about this assumption—if phrases like pot odds and reverse tells, or even traveling blinds and betting limits, cause you to stare off into space with your jaw gone slack—then this isn't the book for you, at least not yet. It's not that this is *that* complex a book. It's just that it addresses the question of how to beat the online game in contrast to strategies used to beat the real world game. If you don't know basic poker, then you'd better go take care of that business first.

If you do know basic poker, then you know that the standard formula for success is selective/aggressive play, in which you enter pots infrequently, but when you do come, you come on strong. In my book, *Killer Poker: Strategies and Tactics for Winning Poker Play,* I describe this strategy as "Go big or go home." Interestingly, this is not a philosophy that applies to online play, for reasons we will look at now.

MINIMIZE YOUR RISK

"A man should never gamble," says the sage, "more than he can stand to lose." This is good advice in all forms of gaming, but it's especially true for Internet poker, where the speed of play and other pitfalls can imperil your bankroll in ways you've never imagined and can't take steps to prevent. Whatever else you do with the information in this book, I hope you'll take this one bit of wisdom to heart: Don't bet big in Internet poker. Why? Because if one of the unavoidable traps of online play happens to trap you, at least it won't trap you or punish you in a financially meaningful way.

Consider this scenario: You're playing hold'em online, and you're dealt A♠ K♠ under the gun. You raise; the guy behind you raises; the guy behind *him* raises; you find yourself taking the flop six ways, with the betting capped. The flop, *mirabile visu,* comes Q♠ J♠ T♠. The crowd goes wild! (Which is to say that you, in the privacy of your own home, go wild, jumping up and down and shouting out your joy.) A raising war breaks out as it becomes apparent that everybody else likes their hand too. In a frenzy of betting, all sorts of cyberchips go into the cyberpot. Glee fills you to the core of your being. You're going to win.

You're going to win big.

And then . . .

Your computer goes dead!

It could be a lightning strike or a terrorist attack or an earthquake or rats gnawing through power lines. Hell, it could even be your six-year-old playing with the plugs. In any event, through no fault of your own, in a manner totally beyond your control, you're taken out of action in a monster hand.

If you've played online already, then you already know that most sites make provisions for this sort of occurrence. The so-called *all-in disconnect* treats your sudden disappearance as an all-in wager. That's good, up to a point, for it means that your investment in the pot up till now is protected. You're going to win all those pre-flop and post-flop bets, and that's not nothing. But also it's not everything. It's not any of the bets that you would have won on the turn and the river when your monkeyfish foes with their lesser straights and flushes blithely bet into your monster. No need to do the math; let's just say that your catastrophic disconnect has cost you half of what you would otherwise have won. How do you like life now?

If you've lost half of a *lot* of money, you feel real bad. If you've lost half of a *little* money, you feel a lot less bad.

All computer users, writers especially, know what it's like to endure a computer crash at the worst possible time. Many screenwriters have tales of woe about a terrific, brilliant script or scene that was lost because their computer suffered a sudden meltdown and they, foolishly, had not backed up their work. Has it happened to me? Of course it's happened to me. But only once. After that, I learned to save my work frequently, almost obsessively, in fact, so that if (when) my computer does next crash, I'll only lose the last ten minutes of creative output, and not the whole day's work.

In fact, I think I'll back up this file now.

There. Safe.

This is called *minimizing risk,* and it is a vital part of your online play strategy. The sad fact is that sooner or later you *will* experience a catastrophic disconnect. It will happen when you least want it to, and it will cost you at least some theoretical profit, I promise. If that theoretical profit is *huge, huge, huge,* you will rail and curse the gods. But if that theoretical profit is a not-that-significant sum of money, you will be much better equipped, on an emotional level, to take the setback in stride. And it's absolutely crucial for you to be able to take such setbacks in stride, for they are an absolute fact of online poker life.

"A man should never gamble more than he can stand to lose." Especially online, where the reasons for losing may have nothing to do with the way you play the hand. Never play online for life-changing sums of money. Put some discretionary income into play, fine. But don't bet the house;

don't even bet a mortgage payment. It's bad enough to lose fair and square, but if you play online for any length of time, I promise there will come a time when you lose unfairly, possibly even unsquarely. Maybe, as in the example described previously, you'll lose a connection at a key moment in a key hand. Maybe your online poker provider will go broke and abscond with your hard-won funds. It could happen—hell, it's happened more than once already in the short history of Internet poker. Maybe you'll fall victim to garden-variety online collusion. Anyone who thinks that the only losses they'll absorb online will be the normal losses of normal poker play is just not paying attention. Sorry, but it's true. Do not be this person.

When you play poker online, you want to play your best. You want to focus all your concentration and mental energy on playing perfect poker, Killer Poker, just as you would in any real-world poker game. But how can you do this if, in the back of your mind, you're worried about the solvency of your online poker provider or the integrity of your Internet connection or the honesty of your unseen online foes? You can't. You will, inevitably, play less than perfectly if worry *in*fects your thinking.

Worry will naturally infect your thinking less if there's less real money at stake. So minimize your online investment. Do this one thing, and your online experience will be a much more rewarding and enjoyable one, I promise. It may even be a more profitable experience, because what you lose in betting limit you gain in tranquility and focus.

Suppose you want to go to a nightclub in a bad neighborhood. You can't *not* go to the nightclub; your favorite band is playing. But you can't *not* have the nightclub be in a bad neighborhood; it is where it is. So what do you do? You strip your wallet of excess cash and credit cards. You leave your swanky jewelry at home. You drive the old Pinto instead of the new Jaguar. That way, if your nightmare scenario comes true, if unscrupulous thugs hold you up for everything you've got, they'll get less than they otherwise would. You have minimized your risk. You've also improved your state of mind. In the likeliest scenario, you *won't* get rolled. You'll go to the nightclub, enjoy the band, and come home with no worse consequences than a hangover the next morning. But if you've prepared for the worst, you'll be much more likely to enjoy the event in the event that the worst doesn't come to pass.

Same with online poker, only the issue is not just enjoyment but also performance. If you're constantly worried about negative outcomes, you simply won't play your best. And since some negative outcomes are unavoidable online, you can't afford this worry. Which means that you must minimize your investment, and thus minimize its mental impact on you. I'm not saying that online poker is the equivalent of a nightclub in a bad neighborhood, but, okay, I am.

At the end of the day, this point may be moot, because most sites don't have super-big games to begin with. As of this writing, the largest limit games routinely spread online are $20–$40. Of course there's pot-limit and no-limit action as well, and in those games you could certainly drop a wad if you weren't careful. So *be* careful. Don't let your greed for online glory outweigh your responsible approach to a form of gambling whose every technical and tactical aspect you simply can't control.

MOST PLAYERS LOSE ONLINE

If you plan to play poker online, you'd better understand this truth: The majority of people who play poker online lose money in the long run. Why? Because the majority of people who play poker *period* lose money in the long run, whether in cyberspace or in b&m (brick and mortar) cardrooms and casinos.

Is this true? Yes, it's true. In the first place, most players don't take time to learn how to play the game properly, and thus the casual poker enthusiast routinely falls victim to the genuinely skilled and educated and dedicated player. In the second place, every poker room, in the real world and cyberspace alike, charges players to play. This charge, the *rake,* happens to good players and bad players alike, so that if every player were equally skilled, with each winning the same size pots with the same frequency, *all players would lose* in the long run. Since not all players are, in fact, equally skilled, the vast majority of unschooled players end up paying off both the house and the talented few. The combination of laziness and relentless raking trends most players toward negative net outcomes.

Most players don't like to admit this. They go to great lengths to deny it. They tell themselves (and their spouses, friends, dogs, clergy, anyone else who will listen) that they're "break-even or better," even though they don't have the statistical evidence to back up their claim. If they play mostly in the b&ms, it's easy enough for them to perpetuate this falsehood. They "forget" how much they bought in for. They "forget" a trip or two to the ATM. They let anecdotal memory of big wins wash away recollection of unpleasant and all-too-frequent losing sessions. Real-world poker is a fuzzy environment where distinctions between poker bankrolls and "other money" can be blurred, and all sorts of denials can take root and grow.

Online, this lie is not nearly so easy to perpetrate. Every player must take certain steps in order to put real money into play on the Internet. These steps leave a statistical trail—one that's easy to verify and damnably difficult to deny. Face it: If last week you moved $1,000 into www. nakedpoker.com (not a real site, so don't bother looking), and this week you don't have it, you'll have a hard time convincing yourself or your spouse, clergy or dog that the money went to gas, lodging, or food.

Internet poker, then, throws the fact of our losses into sharp, undeniable relief. This has a startling effect on some players. If they fancy themselves winners in the b&m environment, and then find themselves losing online, they often feel perplexed. Worse, they feel paranoid. Knowing (imagining) themselves to be winning players, they can't believe that they have suddenly lost all their skills. Groping for an alternative explanation, they conclude that the online game is somehow rigged against them, and this is why they lose.

Wrong. They lose because they're generally not great players. They lose because they don't make the strategic adjustments required of Internet poker. They lose because they lose focus, or don't treat their outcomes seriously, or otherwise fall into the plentiful and common traps of online play. They lose—only now they have to face that fact, because the harsh reality of their depleted online bankroll is staring them in the face.

So then, we have this fact: The majority of online players will lose money, just as the majority of any poker population will. Your job, then, is to be in the minority. To achieve this goal, you will have to pay close attention to the nuances of the online game. You'll have to surrender your reliance on certain skills, such as reading face tells and body tells, and increase your expertise in other areas, such as interpreting statistical data. You'll need an honest self-appraisal of your poker skills and a willingness to adapt those skills in new and surprising ways. Online play requires, in short, hard work. If you're not willing to do this work, you must simply accept your place in the majority and be content to let your money flow to the skilled and diligent few, and to the house.

This is not acceptable to most players, nor should it be. After all, you work hard for the money that you choose to invest in online play. It stands to reason that you wouldn't want to pee it away if you didn't have to. Well, you don't have to, not if you're willing to admit your limitations going in. So if you find yourself losing money online, don't be so quick to blame "the system." Don't assume that you're being cheated; you're probably not. Be prepared to say to yourself, "It may be that I'm not quite as good at this thing (yet) as I need to be." Be prepared to improve. And then you can be one of the few who reap what the hapless many may sow.

ONLINE PLAY HAS A UNIQUE EMOTIONAL IMPACT

Whether you realize it or not, you take steps to prepare yourself for b&m poker play. If there's a drive involved in the journey to your poker destination, you spend time on that drive thinking about the type of game you're likely to find, how long you plan to play, who you're going to en-counter, and a host of other factors. Even if you're only traveling across a casino from your hotel room to the poker room, you're involved in a change of space, and this phys-ical transition naturally brings about a mental transition as well. You go from "not playing poker" to "playing poker." You enter a poker frame of mind.

Online is different. It's a snap to get into a game. You can go from cleaning the cat box to posting a blind in the time it takes to click "deal me in." Hell, you can even clean the cat box and play poker at the same time. The fact of this easy transition from *not playing* to *playing* means that the time of your mental and emotional preparation may be diminished to the point of nonexistence. You can find yourself involved in big hands and crucial decisions before you're ready in any meaningful sense.

I'm not suggesting that you must leave your house and go walk around the block before you settle in for an online session, although that certainly wouldn't be a bad idea. Even five minutes alone with your thoughts will help you launch your online session in the right frame of mind. Why would you not take that time? Are you that impatient to get your virtual cards in the air? Then you have a problem with patience, and this problem is only exacerbated by the speed and ease with which you can become involved in on-line play.

It goes deeper than this. When you go to play poker in a b&m, you're entering a *poker environment*. Everything about the place says poker: the players, the table and chairs, the dealers, cards, cash, and chips. Being in a poker environment helps you enter a *resource state* appropriate to the task at hand. Resource states are familiar frames of mind in which certain sorts of thinking take place. An artist or a writer, for instance, only starts to work productively when he enters his *creativity resource state*, the frame of mind in which his ideas most freely flow. Likewise, many poker players are not at their sharpest until they have warmed up, become mentally reacquainted with poker's decisions and patterns of thought. When you put yourself in a poker environment, your mind naturally shifts into its poker-playing resource state.

But this shift takes time. Ask any writer who has stared at a blank screen or any painter who has stared at a blank canvas, and they'll tell you that nothing happens until the juices start to flow. Same with poker. You have to be in the game environment for at least a little while before your poker juices start to flow. When you jump from cleaning the cat box to posting the blind, the shift into your effective resource state can lag quite far behind.

Many players thus find themselves mentally unprepared for online play on both a conscious and an unconscious level. They haven't done the *conscious* preparation work which gets them mentally ready for the challenges and choices they're about to face, nor have they made the *unconscious* transition from another mental state into the poker resource state.

You can see where this is leading. If you make the jump into online play without proper mental preparation, you run the risk of playing badly to start, and losing early money as a result. This would be like taking a long flight to Las Vegas and throwing yourself into a game before you'd had a chance to recover from jet lag or other rigors of the trip. Maybe you go to Vegas only a couple times a year; online play offers you the opportunity to make this mistake of impatience *every time you play*. No player can afford to squander the quality of the first half hour of his session, every single session, and hope to be net plus over time.

To guard against this, you must be prepared to, well, be prepared. Treat every session as a serious affair. Take a moment, or two or three, to collect your thoughts and plan your strategy before jumping into a game. The mistakes you don't make early are ones you don't have to overcome later.

Here's another emotional danger of online play: the visceral impact of poker is less potent online than it is in the b&m. If you lose a big pot in a cardroom, you see those chips go away and you see your stack get smaller. Online, the only thing that changes is a number on a screen. It's all too easy to treat that number as insignificant, all too easy not to feel the loss, deep down in your gut where it counts. When that happens—when you disconnect from the emotional impact of losing—you run the risk of not caring whether you win or lose.

Now keep in mind, being emotionally involved in the game is not the same as experiencing fear. A lot of players, in any poker environment, have the problem of fearing to lose. You might feel that the natural emotional disconnect of online poker would free you from that fear. But draw the distinction between *not fearing* and *not caring*. When you don't care about the outcome, sloppy play, poor decision making, and stunning losses can result.

It's easy to forget you're playing for real money online; thus it is easy to become careless about what you do. This underscores once again the need for a serious approach to the recreation of online play. It's a given that you will enjoy online poker more if you play well and win money. Neither of these things will happen if you don't attend to the real emotional differences between online play and the b&m experience.

IT'S HARD TO PLAY YOUR BEST GAME ONLINE

When you play poker in a cardroom or casino, you're not just emotionally prepared; you're also *behaviorally* prepared. In service of perfect poker, you attend to all sorts of useful little procedures. You put on your poker face, so that you present the image you wish to present to the other players at the table. You increase your awareness of other people, drawing information about your opponents through your eyes and ears, and collating this endless stream of sensory input into hypotheses about tendencies and tells. You note the number of chips you have (counting and recounting them, perhaps) and consider your stack size relative to others at the table. You monitor play at the other tables, to see whether a richer opportunity awaits you elsewhere. You do all of these things automatically, because you're in a poker environment, and that very environment, through habit and long experience, instructs you to do so. Immersed in a rich sensory stew of poker, you find it easy and natural to enter your zone of quality poker and play your best game.

Not so online. Sure, you're still getting visual and auditory cues, but these cues are *representational,* not real. And I'm not talking about the difference between real-world and online tells; there definitely are online tells, and I'll get to them in due time. No, what I'm talking about is that when you're playing poker online, your poker information comes from a limited source—your computer screen. You're *accessing* a poker environment, but you're not *immersed* in it, and the difference will impact your play.

Then there's the matter of focus. As previously mentioned, everything in the b&m environment reminds you that you're *playing poker.* You're in a place where poker is played, surrounded by other people doing the very same thing, in a room dedicated to that pursuit. But when you play online, sitting in your swivel chair in front of your computer, you're in a place that's only used for poker on a part-time basis. Looking around my home office, I see a place where I write my books, balance my checkbook, talk on the phone, send and receive e-mail, read, listen to music, watch TV, play Hackey Sack, and sometimes sleep. Looking around your home office or cozy computer nook, what kind of space do you see?

As an exercise, take a moment and list all the uses you

put that space to. You will be astounded to discover what a tiny fraction of your time in that space could possibly be devoted to poker.

Whatever else it may be, then, your Internet poker terminal is in no sense a pure poker environment. It has dozens of distractions built in, and these distractions will definitely conspire to erode your focus. When you play poker in a place where you're used to doing other things, it's hard to bring your best concentration to bear. The impact of this is greatest during your first days of online poker play, but it never completely goes away.

If you don't yet have long experience playing poker online, you also have a great deal of unlearning to do. Many of the strengths and skills that you rely upon to succeed in the real world simply will not serve you in cyberspace. I, for instance, have collected countless extra bets by trading on my playful image. With a natural tendency to do outrageous things anywhere anyway, I parlay this tendency into "antics" at the poker table, which obscure the true quality or nature of my play. I call it "lulling my foes into a false sense of stupidity," but it's not a skill that serves me well online, for the obvious reason that they can't *see* me dressed like a leprechaun or tearing up a twenty-dollar bill and swallowing the pieces with my orange juice. Nor, for that matter, can I see their hands shake when they have big tickets.

This, then, is another reason why you don't naturally bring your best game to the online experience. You don't have your usual bag of tricks at your disposal, and it takes time and training to fill a new bag. Especially when you're first starting out, you may find yourself feeling vaguely hamstrung by what you can't do online.

You don't have to feel vaguely hamstrung. You can feel articulately and specifically hamstrung, if you just spend a moment to explore the issue more fully. With that in mind, I'd like you to do another exercise. (If you've read my other books, you know that I'm big on exercises, especially written ones, which allow you to investigate your play in a thorough, logical, and concrete way.) Catalog what you perceive as the strengths of your game and ask yourself whether you think each strength will serve you online. I'll start you off.

POKER STRENGTH OR SKILL	LIKELY TO BE AN ASSET ONLINE	
	Yes	No
Calculating odds		
Image play		
Card memory		

Did you do the exercise? If not, I urge and exhort you to go back and do it now. With this book, as with all tomes that try to teach you something, you only get out of the experience what you put into it. So do this exercise. In fact, do them all. They cost little enough in terms of time, and only slightly more in terms of frank introspection, but in all cases pay real dividends when you play. In case you hadn't heard, no poker player can hope to excel if he's not willing to be honest and articulate with himself about himself. And while it's easy to be honest about your strengths ("I project a damn good table image!") you may find it harder to be honest with yourself about your failings ("My voice cracks when I'm bluffing"). But take heart! Some of those failings may actually be failings no more once you get online. (Who cares whether your voice cracks, e.g.) So let's do the exercise again, only this time list some holes or leaks in your play and speculate on whether those leaks are likely to hurt you online.

POKER FLAW OR WEAKNESS	LIKELY TO BE A LIABILITY ONLINE	
	Yes	*No*
Visible tells		
Tendency to play too loose		
Tendency to go on tilt		

Some of your flaws, then, will actually hurt you less on-line, because the online environment doesn't give them a chance to do damage. For the ones that can hurt you, though, be warned that they can hurt you a good deal more, for the simple reason that you'll see a lot more hands. Whereas a b&m table might throw down 30 hands an hour, you could see twice or even three times that many online. If you do the same thing wrong over and over again in the real world, you'll repeat that mistake a whole lot more online.

Here's another reason you're likely not to bring your best game to the virtual table: *No one is watching!* In the real world, we often make choices based on how we are per-ceived or how we want to be perceived by other players. Many, for example, don't like to get "caught" playing bad hands out of position. We fear the disapproval of our poker peers. Now, one could argue whether this fear is sensible or not, but the fact remains that, in a live game against real people (especially people we know), pure human pride will often keep us from getting out of line. Not so online. Online, you're anonymous. Hiding behind a screen name or an avatar, you can justify all sorts of crazy plays that you wouldn't let yourself get caught dead doing in a real-world game. Draw to an inside straight? Why not? It only costs a bet, and *who's to know?* Run a hopeless bluff? Why not? It probably won't work, but *who's to know?* The fact of this anonymity will blow serious holes in your play if you're not careful. It's amazing how, out there in the b&ms, peer pressure keeps us on the straight and narrow. In cyber-space, that peer pressure is gone, and its absence can have a noticeable negative effect on our play.

Not to beat the dead horse of this, but I really do en-courage you to participate in this book in a meaningfully interactive way. To help you do that, I'll pose this question, just as if I were your high school teacher and this were a pop quiz:

Based on everything you know (or don't yet know) about Internet poker, why do you think you may be unlikely to play this brand of poker at the highest level of your skill? Write down your observations here, or in a separate notebook or journal.

_____

_____

You'll be surprised how much better you play if only you become aware of the reasons that you might not automatically play so well.

EVERYTHING HAPPENS FASTER ONLINE

When you go to play poker at a b&m, you put your name on a sign-up list, and you wait to get a seat. They may have a spot open for you already, in which case you are seated immediately—immediately, that is, except for the time it takes you to convert your cash into chips, rustle up a chair cushion, wait for some player or players to switch seats, wait for your blind, and so on. "Immediately" in this case, can take several minutes.

When you go to play poker on the Internet, you put your name on a sign-up list, and you are seated *immediately*. In the time it takes for some not-very-complex software to load, you will find yourself choosing from among the available seats at the table. You bring your cyberchips with you when you come, so you don't have to flag down any chip runners. You're sitting in your own chair at your own desk, so if you need cushions, you already have 'em. If other players want to change seats, they either did so before you arrived, or they're out of luck now. You may still have to wait for your blind, but even that wait will be a fraction of its real-world equivalent, as a function of the faster play of hands.

And that's just getting into the game. Now think about all the simple "process" things that happen faster in the online realm. Shuffling is done automatically, in nanoseconds. Cards are dealt in the blink of an eye. Bets are placed at mouse-click pace. There's no pot to push. If the pot is split, the calculation is done instantly. There's never a deck change or a dealer change, no wait for players to be seated. All the business of poker happens at breakneck speed online. How do you think this will affect your play?

You'll have much less time to think about things, that's for sure. Suppose you take a bad beat. In the real world, you'll probably have half a minute or a minute (the time it takes the dealer to scramble, shuffle, and deal) to collect your thoughts before you have to make another poker decision. This time may be just what you need to calm down, regain your composure, get over your bad beat, and keep from going on tilt. But take that same beat online, and you're faced with another decision again almost immediately. The emotional fallout from the last hand can carry over much more easily to the next hand, because the next hand is upon you so fast. You may find yourself on tilt before you know it, because you face your next decision literally "before you know it."

There are certain circumstances where the pace of play online can seem infuriatingly slow. Watching another player's time-out clock count down can seem to take an eternity (and make you want to reach out through the phone line and strangle the chowderhead who's slowing down your game). But this lull is only relative to the overall accelerated speed of the online game. It merely points out by exception that online poker is fast beyond fast compared to the real-world game.

Will this have an impact? Of course it will, and not just in terms of tilt risk. It can also make breaks difficult to take. In a real-world game of hold'em or Omaha, for example, if you're moving into early position, you know that it will take at least a few minutes for the blind to reach you, giving you time to go to the bathroom or catch a breath of fresh air or whatever. Online, that blind is never more than moments away. The call to action is continuous. It's hard to tear yourself away. And it's easy to experience mental fatigue. You see hand after hand after hand, with no respite. Things start to blur.

The composition of tables changes so quickly, too, and this has an impact as well. If you're playing $3–$6 dealer's choice at the Player's Club in Ventura, California, a nice little three-table joint with a crew of reliable regulars, you're likely to see the same faces, or mostly the same faces, throughout a whole evening's play. That kind of thick consistency never happens online. Your foes come from all over the world. They come and go in seconds. You may not even have noticed they were there. Just when you've drawn a reliable bead or read, they vanish into thin air.

This accelerated pace of play is not all bad, of course. If the hands are coming at you fast and furious, it does tend to focus your attention and keep your head in the game. There's literally no time for the mind to wander. Also, whatever real edge you have over your opponents will be magnified by the speed of play. If you make better decisions than they do, you want to be involved in as many decision situations as possible. The online environment is a realm of *many* decisions. Get your foes leaning the wrong way and you can keep them off balance for a long and profitable time.

Assuming they'll stick around for that, for another thing you can do very fast online is leave the game. A mere click of the mouse and you're history. And with so many other games going on all over cyberspace, there's very little reason for a player to stay put in an unfavorable situation. It's not like they'll have to wait long for a seat elsewhere. It's not like they have to *drive* anywhere. Thus, you'll find, it's infuriatingly easy for the fishies to wriggle off the hook.

But don't worry. There's plenty of other fishies out there, just waiting for a chance to nibble the bait, for the fast pace of Internet poker is especially appealing to action junkies. Whatever real poker skills they may have are mitigated by their desire to *just ... be ... involved*. Some extremely bad players actually prefer online poker to the b&m experience precisely because the pace of play is so fast. If they have to fold—which they can't *stand* to do—they know that this hand will end and another will start very soon.

So the speed of online poker can be both a blessing and a curse. The effect it has on you will depend largely on your approach to the game. If you're just in it for the buzz, well, you'll get plenty of buzz, but you probably won't make money. If you're looking for profit, and you're prepared to adjust your game to the accelerated pace, then you may find a hospitable home online.

BOREDOM IS YOUR NUMBER ONE FOE

This true fact of Internet poker may seem a little counterintuitive at first. How, one may wonder, can the game be boring when the pace of play is so fast? Who has *time* to be bored? You'd be surprised. If you've never played online before, you *will* be surprised. Even though you know that the next hand is only seconds away, those seconds can seem like hours. Why should this be?

For one thing, the very speed of Internet poker creates its own expectation for more speed. Once you become accustomed to the pace, a certain subjective reality sets in. Fast isn't fast anymore. You find yourself frustrated by any little delay. Periods of time that are insignificant in the b&m's become intolerable online. You had to wait *how long* to get a seat? *Two minutes?! Unconscionable!* That player took how long to fold her hand? *Ten seconds?! Unbearable!*

But the biggest reason for online poker boredom concerns the way your mind receives information about the game. When you play in the real world, immersed in the total poker environment, everything you see and hear and feel contributes to your overall understanding of the scene. There is abundance of nuance, from the way your opponents say, "Check" to the feel of your chips in your hand as you shuffle them. You are, in a sense, in an ocean of poker— on a sensory level, a richly satisfying place to be.

It is different online. All your information comes from one source, the computer screen right in front of your eyes. Even if you have all your audio options turned on, you're getting at best a dozen different pre-programmed sounds. No matter how textured the graphics of your online site (and some of them are pretty good) you're still just looking at representations on a screen. Instead of a sensory ocean, you find yourself sitting by a single stream, a data stream. The information available to you is not rich and it's not complex. In this situation, it's easy to feel understimulated, uninvolved . . . in a word, bored.

This boredom is very dangerous. It can cause you to do

many things detrimental to your play. It makes you chase hands with bad cards because you can't stand to be out of action. It makes you turn your attention elsewhere, so that you miss valuable information about your foes. Worst of all, it motivates you to fill your environment with other sources of information (distractions) such as television, music, or telephone calls. To fight the enemy of boredom, you must be content to stare at the screen, the whole screen, and nothing but the screen for all the hours that you play. Can you do this? Will that be enough sensory input for you? If it's not, then you have a problem.

A problem, alas, that I share.

As someone who could have been a poster child for attention deficit disorder, I long ago discovered a simple truth about myself: the one thing I want to do more than anything is many things at once. In a nightmare of overstimulation, here's how I might find myself fighting boredom during an online poker session:

> *I'm playing two different games on two different sites. I have a word processing program open and I'm taking notes on my opponents and also recording my own thoughts and observations about the game. Across the room, not quite outside my field of vision, there's a baseball game on TV. But the sound is off, because I'm listening to Steely Dan on the stereo, trying for the umpteenth time to figure out who Katy lied to, and why. I have a headset telephone, so my hands are free to type and click as I chat with a friend who knows nothing about poker and can't understand why I'm alternatively so animated (I won!) and anguished (I lost). I'm drinking coffee (maybe even Irished). There's a yo-yo in my desk drawer that I toss from time to time. The printer on my desk is spitting out pages of my latest script. Now the fax machine comes to life, and I deal with some corre-*

spondence from a client overseas. Of course I'm answering my e-mail. I'm answering the doorbell too, if it rings. Scratching my dog behind her ears. Drawing doodles on a scratch pad. Clipping my nails. Nursing a sneeze.

That's almost enough stimulation for me. Almost. . . .

If you think I'm exaggerating, trust me I'm not. Hell, I'm playing poker online even as I write these words (and playing again even as I edit them). I'm not recommending this as a strategy by any stretch of the imagination. I'm merely pointing out that many online players—even guys who write about it—run the risk of being bored, and the further, bigger risk, of fighting that boredom with other stimulation sources.

Now, jot down a truthful list of all the things *you've* done while playing poker online.

_____

_____

If you've not yet played online, survey your home office or computer nook and list all the possible sources of distraction that could threaten your efforts.

_____

_____

Boredom *can* be fought. Soon we'll discuss weapons to use against it. But don't imagine that the answer to boredom is distraction. That's a deadly combination. It'll eat your bankroll alive.

ONLINE PLAY WILL NOT NECESSARILY IMPROVE YOUR REAL-WORLD PERFORMANCE

A lot of people get into Internet poker in the mistaken belief that it will help them fine-tune their poker play and make them monsters at the table in the b&ms. Nothing could be further from the truth. (Okay, some things could be further from the truth—for instance, looking at a picture of supermodel Marloes van der Heijden on the Internet will not magically make her appear at my door.) While virgin players will gain some useful understanding of poker's structure and rules, and even a sense of relative hand values, online poker differs so much from real-world play that, in general, what you learn online will not translate into triumph in the real world.

Some reasons for this are self-evident. As we have already discussed, the kind of information you glean in a b&m poker environment is much different from, and much more rich and varied than, the data you collect online. Suppose you become triumphant in the online game. You still know nothing about how to search body language for tells, or about how to use your table image to manipulate your opponents.

And again, real-world poker makes demands on a player that Internet poker does not. If you drive to play poker, you're likely to be in the game for some number of hours. (If you fly, you could be at it for days.) Stamina, then, is an asset to your play in the real world. Online, if you get tired, you quit. In the b&ms, if you get tired, you're much more likely not to quit. How will a dozen hit-and-run sessions online prepare you for the rigors of the real-world marathon?

On the other hand, the accelerated pace and self-induced

distraction problems of Internet play can teach players valuable lessons in concentration and patience. If you are able to play a solid, tight game on the Internet, where the temptation to play too loose is so great, it's possible that the discipline you acquire through this exercise will serve you well in the real world, too.

But it's more likely that if you learn how to beat the online game, you will have only learned how to beat the online game. A lot of your success in Internet poker depends on your ability to manipulate certain kinds of data—data that are not available in the b&m realm. For example, online play offers you the possibility of keeping extensive written records about your opponents' performance, records you can update, and also refer to, while you play. If online player *TulsaChronic* check-raises on the turn with a flush draw on board, you can go back and examine your book on this player and see what she's done in the past in similar situations before you decide to call, raise, or fold. Try this in a b&m cardroom—*"Time, please, while I leaf through my notebook"*—and see how far you get!

Skill at storing and interpreting data, then, becomes a weapon in your arsenal of online play, a weapon that you can't use nearly as effectively in the real world. Yes, you can keep a mental book on the players you face, but the physical book, the kind of data bank you can assemble and refer to in online play, is not generally available to the real-world player. You have to rely on your memory—a memory which may actually have atrophied through use of the online crutch of visible, written records.

Your strength at online play, then, can cause you to overestimate or misinterpret your overall poker skill. You can believe yourself to be an excellent player in general, even though your record of success exists only within the confines of online play. To stretch a metaphor to the snapping point, just because you know how to water ski doesn't mean you can snow ski too.

In sum, beginning poker players can get a certain amount of educational value out of playing poker on the Internet, the same sort of value they'd get from a decent piece of poker simulation software. And whatever your skill level, you can enhance and increase your skills *in the online environment,* and make yourself a more formidable foe *in that environment.* But if you think that logging a thousand hours at www.worldseriesofcyberspace.com is going to prepare you to triumph at the World Series of Poker, you're probably leading yourself astray.

It's not entirely out of the question that you would lead yourself astray on purpose. People playing poker, especially those who are playing and losing, often find themselves looking for reasons to keep playing poker, or to play more poker, or to play for higher stakes. If you've got a jones for Internet poker, you might very well find yourself justifying that jones in the name of "sharpening your skill set." This is, of course, a cheap rationalization and a threat to those who indulge in it.

So I return once again to the fundamental question: Can you tell the truth about yourself to yourself? Win or lose, are you able to look at your participation in online poker and say, "I'm doing this for fun or for modest profit, but in any event I'm doing it because I *want* to, not because I *have* to"? Can you play poker online for clear-eyed, conscious reasons, or must you dress up your involvement with transparent lies? If it's the latter, then I submit to you that you may have the sort of problems that playing more Internet poker will only make worse.

ONLINE PLAY MAGNIFIES MISTAKES

By accelerating and compressing the pace of play, online poker causes bad players to play worse—sometimes much worse. If there are holes in your game, and you do not take steps to fix them, you can anticipate losing a lot of money in online play.

Part of this, as you have already seen, is simple mathematics. If you're playing twice as many hands per hour, your overall quality of play will reveal itself twice as fast. This is something that people rarely take into account in card-rooms and casinos: the leisurely pace of play actually keeps bad players from hurting themselves too badly. They just don't have enough time to do that much damage. Online, the pace is anything but leisurely; it's breakneck.

And break-wallet, too, because the amount of time you have to make proper choices is truncated. Sure, you can take your time online. You can pause to study your decision, *up to a point*. But soon you'll see the time-out counter ticking down onscreen, warning you that you have 20 . . . 15 . . . 10 . . . 5 seconds to call, raise, or fold. Nor can you ask the dealer for more time; when you run out of time, you'll be treated as all-in, or in certain circumstances folded out, whether you like it or not. Under pressure of that sort of deadline, you're at risk for all sorts of rash and ill-considered actions. And even without the pressure of the deadline to stimulate your (foul) play, the fact that everyone around you is acting so quickly will naturally make you tend to act quickly, too. Before you know it, you're making decisions you'd ordinarily never make, just because you're not taking the time to contemplate your options.

Further accelerating the pace of play is the fact that many online games are played shorthanded. If you get in a game with just three or four players, you can easily find yourself on a merry-go-round spinning wildly out of control. The common decisions of poker—compounded, perhaps, by your unfamiliarity with shorthanded play—confront you much more frequently, over and over and over again.

Consider this example. Richard is a pretty good all-around poker player. He's selective-aggressive in most respects and doesn't have too many gaping holes in his game. One identifiable flaw in his play is his play of blinds. He defends too liberally pre-flop, and surrenders any flop he doesn't hit. Savvy opponents know this; they know that they can make money by raising into his blind and then betting any board that looks the slightest bit scary. In the b&ms, this flaw doesn't hurt Richard all that much. He typically plays in full games and thus sees maybe three or four big blinds an hour. If he plays one or two of them incorrectly, this leak costs him at most a few bets per hour.

But in his online incarnation, *RichardTheLionheart,* he often finds himself playing in shorthanded games. Instead of defending three or four blinds an hour, he's now exposing his weakness as many as 30 times per hour. A tolerable leak in live play has become a monstrous sinkhole online. Poor Richard.

Why does poor Richard allow himself to play shorthanded if he knows he is at such risk? In the first place, he may not know he *is* at risk. It's the nature of many mistakes to be invisible to their victims; Richard may think he plays his blinds just fine, thank you very much. Second, if Richard is like most online players, he doesn't mind shorthanded play; in fact, he likes it. He has gotten used to the accelerated pace of play and would rather be in action than not. There's even the possibility that Richard *only* plays shorthanded, or even only heads-up, because he fears online collusion and reasons that playing shorthanded mini-mizes this threat; that playing one-on-one eliminates it al-together.

Poor, as they say, Richard.

It's a curious phenomenon of online poker that people who wouldn't be caught dead playing shorthanded in the real world actually gravitate toward shorthanded games on-line. Shorthanded play is bliss for action junkies: Stripped of all the normal social aspects of sitting around a poker table with other human beings, the online version of the game offers the distilled thrill of pure action, pure buzz. In a full game, a reasonable player will throw away the major-ity of his hands, and then have to sit waiting patiently for his chance to play again. In a shorthanded game, the player who throws away a reasonable number of hands is going to be back in action that much more quickly. If *action* is your inducement, then shorthanded play is the place you want to be.

A place, alas, where your mistakes are magnified and multiplied.

But don't forget that your strengths are magnified too. Suppose you're not poor Richard, but rather the savvy ad-versary who has identified this whole hole in Richard's play. You would naturally seek the opportunity to play shorthanded against Richard, and if you could get that op-portunity, you could punish him relentlessly, just on the margin of the mistakes he makes in playing his blinds.

All of which underscores a fundamental truth of poker: good players beat bad players in the long run. It just so happens that, online, the long run arrives much, much faster. Thus we can expect those who lose to lose more on-line.

And so you have another reason to tread cautiously as you enter the online realm. No matter how good a player you think you are, chances are there are problems with your play that you deny, or even actually know nothing about. If you throw yourself into online poker without thoroughly and critically examining your play, you will most likely fall victim to the draconian reality of online play: for players with limited skills or flawed decision-making ability, it definitely makes a bad situation worse.

2

THE MECHANICS OF THE THING

♧ ♤ ◇ ♡

This chapter examines the practical matter of getting signed up with an online poker site and finding your way around once you're there. If you're already familiar with online poker functionality, by all means feel free to skip this section. If not, stick around while we take a closer look.

YOUR COMPUTER AND CONNECTION

To play poker on the Internet you will need, at minimum, a computer with Internet access. The computer should be as fast and powerful as possible, so that it can handle the demands of running Internet poker programs without freaking out, freezing up, or hanging you out to dry. Here are the typical system requirements for downloading and using Internet poker software:

- Windows 95 or above
- 100-MHz Pentium or faster CPU with at least 32 MB of RAM

- Screen resolution of at least 800 by 600 pixels with 256 colors
- 6 MB of free disk space

As with most software applications, strive to have a generous margin for error. The more processor speed, memory, and disk space for the program, the less likely it is that the program will get cranky and give you a hard time.

All other things being equal, I recommend that you use a PC rather than a Mac for Internet poker play. This is no prejudice against Apple products on my part. It's just that on some sites, the PC game is, literally, the only game in town. Here, for example, is what Paradise Poker has to say on the subject:

Currently there is only a Windows version available; there is no Mac/Linux/Java/etc. version. It's our understanding that Paradise Poker games online work well on a Mac running either SoftWindows or VirtualPC, but we can't offer technical support for either of those two products.

So there you go.

In terms of Internet access, you have the usual choices: plain vanilla telephone dial-up, DSL, T-1, and cable or satellite modem. Though dial-up modems were state of the art for Internet access mere years ago, they seem quite slow and almost quaint by today's standards for speed and reliability. DSL in particular, with its always-there, always-on characteristic, is an attractive option for the online poker fan: your next session is only a mouse click away, and you don't even have to wait for the dial-up connection to do its thing. So, again, all other things being equal, opt for DSL or one of its speedy cousins over plain vanilla dial-up.

This may seem self-evident. Of course you want fast, effective, and reliable computer hardware and Internet access; who wouldn't? But it's a point worth stressing just the same. Dropped connections and frozen software are infuriatingly common facts of online poker life. By upgrading your system and access, you at least minimize the chances of these problems originating at your end.

If you're having trouble justifying the expense, consider that inferior computers or Internet access can actually have a negative impact on your win rate. Suppose you have a dial-up connection. Forgetting the fact that it's slow, what if it's just not reliable? If you suffer frequent disconnects while playing online, you are bound to become frustrated. That frustration will definitely color the decisions you make, and not in a positive way. So if you're serious about online poker, consider upgrading those parts of your computer system involved in the play of the game. Yes, it may cost you some money up front, but if it minimizes glitches, and the attendant frustration of same, it can save you many bets, and thus much money, in the long run.

Like you need an excuse to upgrade your toys. But anyway, now you have one.

YOUR ONSCREEN IDENTITY

I don't, I assume, need to tell you how to download and install a new piece of software on your computer, but if I did, my advice would be, "Follow the instructions on-screen and let the computer do its thing." Once you have the software installed, you'll need to register as a player and set up an online identity. Again, from a practical point of view this is just a matter of answering questions as they are asked and filling out the forms as you go.

At some point in the sign-up process, you'll be asked to

select your on-screen name. This is the name by which you will be identified to other players in the game, and it's worth taking a moment in advance to think about what your nickname should be. Before we go any further, I'd like you to jot down a few possibilities either here or in your notebook. I'm going to show you in a second why your first choice might not be your best choice after all.

POSSIBLE SCREEN NAMES

JVplayspoker
MrBadExample
Clueless Parade

Some players take a straightforward approach in creating their on-screen identities. If your name is Nick and you live in Toronto and you don't have an overabundance of imagination, you might come up with *TorontoNick* or *NickfromToronto* or (if you're feeling especially clever today) *Nickoronto*. There's nothing wrong with these choices, except that they do nothing to take advantage of the (minimal) strategic opportunity that selecting a screen name offers. For instance, you could call yourself *BigFish* or *AnyTwoWillDo,* and by such a choice hope to have your foes underestimate the threat you pose. On the other hand, you may wish to present a more imposing image, and so you'd select a more formidable moniker, like *KillerPoker* or *WSOP Champ*. Most of your opponents, of course, will take such self-deprecating or self-aggrandizing declarations with a grain of salt, as well they should. Players learn in short order to discount the fierce—*RaiseWithNothing!*—and the foolish—*WhatBeatsWhat?*—alike. That's why I think that neither the straight choice nor transparent reverse psychology is your best bet.

Instead, do this: choose a name that gives nothing away. Give no hint as to your age, gender, geographical location, level of expertise, or philosophy of play. You might find it fun to call yourself *Hold'emKing,* but if you do that, you betray a predilection for hold'em, which may not serve you well when you decide to jump over into a stud game. Likewise, while you may find it sexy to call yourself *StripPoker-Gal,* why identify yourself as a woman to a poker community that assumes, rightly or wrongly, that women players are more easily attacked?

Unless, of course, you're lying.

You may be a 250-pound steam fitter from Sweden, representing yourself as *90poundNancy* from Nebraska. And who knows, you might even be believed. Whether you're believed or not, you have given away no real information about yourself, and that's the key consideration.

In my experience, most people don't lie. Their screen names are a genuine reflection of their gender, area of interest, or at least their names. *Angelo23* is probably someone really named Angelo. He may be a Michael Jordan fan, as Jordan's number was 23. Or he may be part of the timeless Illuminatus conspiracy, for the number 23 has deep mystical significance to those in the esoteric know. *Backgammon* is probably someone with an interest in other forms of gaming besides poker. *MrPink* is a Quentin Tarantino fan. At least that's what I assume, and I may be totally wrong about all these assumptions. It may be that all of these players are much more devious than I give them credit for. But people will make assumptions, and you should take that fact into account. Over time, your choice of screen name probably won't make a huge money difference, but why give anything away? Keep information about yourself to yourself.

Take a moment now and generate a new list of screen identities for yourself. Don't be self-indulgent and don't be cute. Try to come up with names that either reveal nothing about who you really are or else (deftly, not clumsily) lead people's thinking astray. Make up some names, and then ask yourself what assumptions *you* would make about the player behind those names the first time you two crossed paths.

NAME	SIGNIFICANCE
MiataBoy	Favors style over substance
NoChasing	Trying to stay disciplined
WhiteLightWhiteHeat	Lou Reed fan

The truth, again, is that your observant opponents will quickly look past your screen name, and base their appraisal of you on the way you play. Your unobservant opponents, meanwhile, will lose to you for the mere reason of being unobservant. Still, all other things being equal, why give away *any* edge? Most people pick screen names that suit their personalities. I say pick a screen name that suits your goal of winning money playing poker online. It probably won't make a difference in the long run, but if someone gives you one loose call because your screen name induces them to do so, then it's worth the time you took to think it up.

On a related subject, some sites such as www.truepoker. com let you select an avatar before you start to play. An avatar, if you don't know, is a computer-generated character that represents you on-screen to other players in the game. When you sit at a typical table on a site featuring avatars, you'll see cartoon figures that look like cowboys, aliens, riverboat gamblers, Dixie chicks, street thugs, and more. Which avatar should you select for yourself? Again, self-indulgence would dictate that you pick one that represents you in some sense. But in this situation, *un*common sense should apply. Pick an avatar that's about as far from your true nature as you can get. Change your gender—or even your species. Don't let anyone draw a confident connection between who you are and who you appear to be. There's not much to be gained by this kind of deception, but there's absolutely nothing to lose. Who knows? You might even enjoy being an alien for once in your life.

A website that takes avatars in a different direction is www.pokerstars.com. Its software actually allows you to import the graphic image of your choice and lets this image be the representative of your on-screen self. Most people who exercise this option make the obvious choice of pictures of themselves, their dog or hobby, or something else compatible with who they really are. Again, follow the logic of not giving away any information you don't have to. Select an image that's opposite the true you, or just completely irrelevant. Use a grizzly bear or a drawing of the

Eiffel Tower. A photo of Mae West. Whatever. This sort of misdirection is not likely to gain you much, but it costs you nothing, so take the time to make a thoughtful choice. Remember that your goal is not to impress yourself with your cleverness and certainly not to portray yourself accurately to your foes. Your goal is to maximize profit, and in service of that, you give nothing away.

GETTING TO KNOW THE GAME

The Free-Money Option

Once you've downloaded and installed the site's software, and gone through a minimal sign-in procedure, you'll be ready to play—for play money. There's a longer sign-in procedure if you want to play for actual cash dollars, and I'll get to that in a second—but not yet! You don't know your way around the site. You don't know how the tables are set up, how the command buttons function, or anything. It's time to take a tour.

I can't stress this point strongly enough: even though you could theoretically start to play for real money now, *don't do it.* Get to know every site well before you put any real money into play. As a practical matter, make sure that you know enough not to click the "raise" button when you mean to click "fold." If you're going to make this mistake, you want to make it—and learn from it—when the cost of the lesson is zero.

Because the pace of online play is much faster than real-world games, you'll want to get used to that pace. Take the sports car for a test drive before you buy. Learn to make your decisions more quickly, within the frame of the time allowed, using only the information available to you online. Learn how to gather information about your foes before you go to war, and most definitely learn how to do these things while the learning is free.

Many eager (which is to say overeager) online players don't bother with this interim step. They figure that they already know how to play poker and further figure that they'll figure out all the online functions as they go along. Big mistake. Huge. Every online player is at risk for errors of carelessness or ignorance when he or she first starts out—even you. If you lose real money learning the functionality of online play, that's real money you'll have to win back later. Why would you want to dig yourself that hole? Because, heck, it's boring to play for free, right? Who wants to waste that time?

But it's not a waste of time, not if your head's in the right place. The purpose of the free play tables—for a Killer Poker player like you—is not to entertain yourself but to educate yourself. It's also a great place to practice making correct decisions. If you can fold a bad ace at a free-play table, where there would be *absolutely no cost to call,* you're much more likely to be able to lay down that hand correctly when there's real money on the line.

The first choice you face at the free-play tables is, naturally, which table to pick. Most sites offer an array of games at various play-money limits. Try to pick a play-money limit that corresponds to the real-money limit you'll eventually play. You might, for example, be tempted to play pot limit or no limit hold'em at the free tables, but if you have no intention of playing pot limit or no limit for real money, then spend your time at the fixed limit tables where your learning has some relevance.

When you're brought to a play-money table, you may be offered your choice of seats. Some online sites let players select their own position at the table; other sites just put you in the first available seat. Well, you know and I know that seat selection is a critical element of a player's success, so you'll generally want to gravitate toward sites that give you the most flexibility in this area. For now, though, since the point of the free-play option is to familiarize yourself with the site, don't worry too much about where you sit. Just click on an open space and let them deal you in.

Sussing Out the Table

Once you're seated at the table, take a moment to move your cursor around and see what information is available to you. If you hold your cursor over another player's seat position or avatar, for example, you can see their screen name, where they're from (or *claim* they're from), and how much money they have in play. Some sites will even tell you whether their Internet connection is excellent, fair, or poor, a consideration which has, as you will see, at least some significance. On some sites, you don't need to move your cursor to another player's spot to see this information; it's always on display.

Clicking on the dealer's position or the menu button will give you an array of options concerning how you wish to interface with the site. You may want to turn the sound on or off, or the table chat on or off. Again, if you learn how to do these things at the play-money tables, where education is free, you won't have to waste mental energy familiarizing yourself with the site when there's real money on the line. This is no less important than learning what's a qualified low in Omaha/8 or how many cards come on a flop.

The online poker table offers you a wealth of information, based on which you can make strategic play decisions. For instance, the sites tell you exactly, down to the dollar (or play money dollar), how much money each player has. If you see one free play opponent with only 6 chips left while another has 600, which player is more likely to bluff? Just as you would measure stack size when you sit down in a b&m game, you need to take note of how much money your opponents have online. This information is not always easy to retain. Spending time at the free-play table will help you acquire the habit of keeping track of who's ahead and who's behind, which will naturally help you play your game more effectively.

Setting Your Options

Do you want to hear the virtual clatter of virtual chips going into the pot? Do you want to hear computerized voices utter the words *check, call,* or *raise*? Or would you find such sounds a distraction? Over time you'll develop your own set of preferences—that's why they're called preferences— but for now I encourage you to try all the settings all sorts of different ways. This free-play interlude is your chance to experiment. Make the most of it. Don't assume that you like the sound off *or* on. Try it both ways. You may be surprised.

Likewise, most sites offer a chat box, a little window in which you or other players can input text. Much of this chat is limited to abbreviations such as "nh"—nice hand— or "ty"—thank you. Conversations can get spirited, though, and some players will use the chat box to try to put other players on tilt, or induce calls or folds, and so on. For this reason, some players choose to exercise the option of turning off the chat, and thus not be distracted nor influenced by what the other players have to say. This is the cyberspace equivalent of wearing headphones at the table. It may or may not suit you so, again, try it both ways and decide for yourself what works. Similarly, experiment with sending out some lines of chat and see whether it suits you to be talkative online.

Hand Logs

Hand logs are a record of the play of each hand, and thanks to them you can literally save and study each and every hand you play. Some sites offer you the option of recording hand logs, either by downloading them directly to your computer in real time, or by requesting that a copy of the hand history be sent to your e-mail address.

Look at the following sample hand log.

Game Started on Friday, September 31, 2003, at 17:15
Table Foxtrot
Hold'em Play Money 10/20

—Hand #23232323 begins—

Nard receives the dealer button
Venus posts small blind 5
Itschachi posts big blind 10
WKJ posts 10
You are dealt [Qs,5d]
Sigsigsig folds
WKJ checks
Bulldog calls 10
WickedSlice calls 10
Mochajojo folds
OrangeHappyWater raises 20
Nard calls 20
Venus calls 15

Itschachi raises 20
WKJ calls 20
Bulldog calls 20
WickedSlice calls 20
OrangeHappyWater raises 20
Nard calls 20
Venus calls 20
Itschachi calls 10
WKJ calls 10
Bulldog calls 10
WickedSlice calls 10
Flop is dealt [8s, 4c, Qh]
Venus checks
Itschachi bets 10
WKJ folds
Bulldog folds
WickedSlice calls 10
OrangeHappyWater calls 10
Nard raises 20
Venus folds
Itschachi raises 20
WickedSlice calls 20
OrangeHappyWater calls 20
Nard calls 10
Turn is dealt [6c]
Itschachi bets 20
WickedSlice calls 20
OrangeHappyWater calls 20
Nard raises 40
Itschachi raises 40
WickedSlice calls 40
OrangeHappyWater calls 40
Nard calls 20

> River is dealt [Th]
> Itschachi bets 20
> WickedSlice folds
> OrangeHappyWater folds
> Nard calls 20
> Itschachi shows a pair of Kings
> Itschachi's pocket cards were [Kc, Kd]
> Nard mucks [Qc, Jc]
> Itschachi wins $677 play money from main pot
>
> —Hand #23232323 ends—

As you can see, this hand log describes the play of the hand in a certain type of shorthand or code that takes a little getting used to. But it's a skill worth having, and one that's not hard to acquire, so before you leave the free-money tables and venture into the real-money world, be sure to download or request some hand logs. Take some time to study them so that you know what sort of information they offer and how that information is presented. Ask yourself how you would have played the hands if you had held the cards that other players held. It's a good way to learn not just the rhythm of hand logs but also the tendencies of other players.

Pre-Action Buttons

Most sites offer the opportunity to select certain actions in advance. The ability to "act out of turn" and then have your action wait its proper turn is a fact of Internet poker that has no parallel in the real world. It's vital that you familiarize yourself with all of the pre-action buttons before you throw yourself into the real-money fray.

Some pre-action buttons concern general choices about the way you play. You are offered the option, for instance, of auto-posting your blind. This is a handy way to avoid slowing down the action if you happen to be away from your computer for a moment when it's your turn to post the blind. Just make sure you're back in time to play. If you think you'll be away from the table for any length of time (nature calls!) you can click the *sit out next* button, and they'll deal around you until you're ready to resume play.

You also have the option of selecting *muck lost* or *muck losing hands*. Many players neglect to pick this option, and it's a terrible hole in their game. If they're in a hand to the end and they don't win, they end up showing their opponents the cards they went to the river with. *Never do this!* Your first order of business should be to select auto-muck because there's almost never any point in letting your foes know what you folded. Some sites don't offer this global choice—you have to decide in the moment whether to show your losing cards or not. Generally, you never want to show losing cards. There may be times that you do, either for advertising or deception, but those times are rare enough in the real world, and almost nonexistent online. Turn on your auto-muck feature; don't give anything away.

During the course of any given hand, the pre-action buttons give you a chance to get a jump on things by deciding what you plan to do before the action gets to you. While it's tempting to do so, the use of pre-action buttons can actually be a form of online tell and thus should be avoided. Let's say that you're last to act in a $10–$20 hold'em game, and you hold pocket aces. You've raised pre-flop and gotten three callers. The flop comes A-x-x. Here's a typical array of pre-action choices you now will face:

FOLD   *CALL 10*   *RAISE 20*
CHECK/FOLD   *CHECK/CALL*   *RAISE ANY*

You know that you've flopped huge, and you know that you'll likely raise any bet that comes your way. If you click the *raise any* pre-action button, your bet will be announced *the instant the action gets to you*. Observant opponents will realize that you were prepared to raise any bet, conclude that you're sitting on a monster, and get away from a hand they otherwise might have stuck around with. This may seem like a subtle thing, and it is, but it's an example of an online nuance that's absent from real-world play. Spend time with your pre-action buttons while you're still playing for free money and you'll be much less likely to give away this sort of tell when the time comes to play for real.

Sign-Up Boards

Before leaving the free-play area behind, be sure to spend some time in the lobby looking at the sign-up boards for both free-play and real-money games. These boards offer a wealth of information including the type and size of games in play, the number of players in each game, the percentage of players who see the flop, and average pot-size. This information will be vital to you later when you set out to choose the game, limit, and lineup most conducive to your success. You'll want to be well versed in how to access and interpret the data offered to you by every site's sign-up board or lobby. The time you spend here now, acquainting yourself with this functionality, will pay big money dividends later.

For the practice that's in it, spend your first free-play sessions identifying a couple of really terrible players (they won't be hard to find in the free-play area!); then, next time you log on, scan the game boards for the free-play tables and see whether you can locate one more of these easy targets. If you find them, try to join games they're in. If they're in games that are already full, add your name to the waiting list for those games (another element of functionality that you'll want to learn and master). This "fish where the fish are" strategy will be one of your best real-money friends; it'll be good to get the hang of it now.

In the neighborhood of the sign-up boards are also clickable links to the floorman or casino host. These links are usually, but not always, available within the individual games as well. If you ever have a technical problem or a procedural question, or if you think you're the victim of some online hanky-panky, you can contact the floorman or host either by e-mail or by real-time chat and get your issue resolved.

Playing in the free-play portion of any site will give you a wealth of useful information about that site. One thing it's not likely to give you is a lot of education about how people really play poker, for the simple reason that people who aren't playing for real money are not likely to be particularly careful about the choices they make. The incentive for winning is far outstripped by the incentive for staying in action and seeing the hand through. Don't waste a lot of time and energy trying to beat these games. Concentrate on mastering the look-and-feel aspects of the table, and save your strategic thinking for the real money games where the poker players can be counted on to act like, well, like poker players.

Although many sites are similar in functionality, each site has its own bells and whistles, so spend time in the free play area *on each and every site you join.* Don't assume that just because you've familiarized yourself with one site you now understand them all. To take a simple yet horrifying example, suppose one site has this configuration:

RAISE	*CALL*	*FOLD*

And another site's looks like this:

FOLD	*CALL*	*RAISE*

If you're used to playing at site A, then when you jump to site B, you could very well raise when you intended to fold. That's no big deal when you're playing for free, but a tragedy of measurable (in dollars) proportions when it happens in the real-money world.

3

♣ ♠ ♦ ♥

MONEY MANAGEMENT

Moving money into and out of an online poker site involves some logistical concerns and raises some emotional and psychological issues as well. As you shall see, putting money into play online is not so simple as the real-world equivalent of pulling up a chair, plunking down your cash, and declaring, "Deal me in!"

DEPOSITING MONEY

Getting money into the online site of your choice can take anywhere from five minutes to ten days, depending on how you go about it. In all cases, the sites present certain hurdles to the cashing-in process, both to protect themselves from fraud and other sorts of larceny and to protect you from your own atavistic urges.

By the time you get around to putting real money into a site, you will already have created an online identity and password for yourself. From this point forward, the fastest way to hurl yourself into real-money action is to go to the cashier's window, provide the appropriate information about your whereabouts in both the real and the cyber-world, and make a purchase with your credit card.

Some people are reluctant to give out credit card information online. Despite every site's assurances that their servers are secure, folks do fear that their credit card numbers will be nefariously appropriated and used against them for purposes of thievery and mayhem. Though this fear is not entirely unfounded, I think you're much more likely to be rolled at your local ATM than to fall victim to online credit theft. Nevertheless, to assuage your fears in this area, you might consider getting a separate credit card that you use only for online transactions. That way, if you should be victimized, there will be a firewall of sorts between your online credit and the rest of your money. At minimum, fraud against an online-only card is easier to track for the simple reason that your transactions are fewer in number. An added benefit is the natural separation that this card provides between your online poker bankroll and your finances as a whole.

On the other hand, let me ask you a question: Have you ever been the victim of online credit card chicanery? All right, then. Lighten up and move on.

When you purchase cyberchips with a credit card, there are some associated costs to consider. Many sites charge a fee for credit card purchases—2 percent is typical. Though part of me measures that 2 percent against the cost of tipping real-world dealers and thinks it's not such a bad bargain, another part of me just *hates* having to pay $510 to buy $500 in chips online. It's *my* money, I reckon. Why must I pay for the privilege of using my own money? Further, almost all credit card companies consider such purchases to be not purchases at all, but rather cash advances. Banks and other card-issuing companies routinely impose special fees on cash advances, and they also charge interest from the moment the transaction is made. My bank charges $4 for a $500 cash advance, and imposes interest at the usurious rate of 19.99 percent per annum. If I paid back that advance in my normal 30-day billing cycle, I'd pay another $5 in interest, bringing the total cost of my online deposit to roughly $20. Not exactly a bargain, right?

To make matters worse, some banks—Bank of America and Citibank, to name two behemoth examples—no longer allow their credit cards to be used for online gambling transactions of any kind. The reasons for this vary: some institutions fear downstream legal exposure; they don't want to be drawn into lawsuits as accessories to online gaming. Others have decided that the high incidence of fraud, default, and delinquency associated with this class of transaction make it an unsound risk. Still others are engaged in a form of backdoor social engineering, where by making it difficult to use credit cards for online gambling, they hope to stem that tide.

But, hey, it's their money. What are you going to do?

One thing you could do is bag the credit card approach and send a bank draft, cashier's check, or money order directly to the site. This can take some time and some effort, of course, measured in trips to your local bank and in the physical delivery of financial instruments to overseas locations. Then there's the cost: maybe $5 for the bank draft or money order and another $20 or more for delivery by some sort of express courier to ensure timely and secure arrival. Again, no bargain.

Perhaps you'll go the old-fashioned route and wire the money via Western Union. This will cost even more. For example, to send $500 from Los Angeles, where I live, to Costa Rica, corporate home of several online poker sites, would cost $43, as of this writing. There's got to be a better way.

Fortunately, there is. It's a nifty little online service called Fire Pay. Fire Pay, like its brother-in-commerce NETeller, is a sort of financial holding zone on the Internet, a place where you can park your money for subsequent distribution to virtually any online poker portal. To sign up for the FirePays of this world, just visit their websites and follow the online instructions. You will be prompted to enter certain information about your bank account and must then wait several days for the online service to validate that account. They accomplish this by making two tiny deposits (some small number of cents each) into your account and asking you to verify the fact and amount of these deposits. In this way, FirePay guarantees that the account is actually yours and reduces the risk of someone pulling a fast one with your account information.

Once your account has been verified, you're ready to make a deposit, which can also be accomplished quickly and easily at the FirePay, or NETeller site. It will take at least three working days for your funds to clear. When they're officially "in hand" at FirePay or elsewhere, you can then go to your favorite online poker site, visit their cashier, and arrange for a transfer of funds, which will (at last!) take only a matter of moments. Now you're good to go.

Because you have to wait for your account to be verified, and wait again for your funds to transfer into FirePay, you can be facing a lag of more than a week between the time you first put the wheels in motion and the time you're actually able to play for cash money on a site. That's fine. You're in no hurry. Spend that lag time playing for free and getting the site's functionality completely dialed in.

Viewed from a certain perspective, we could compare this lag to the waiting period required of gun owners. Viewed from a certain perspective, we could speculate that the sites don't want your money going into play before you're psychologically and procedurally prepared. Viewed from a certain perspective, this is hogwash. They want your money. They trust you to gamble responsibly (or else they don't care). The system just precludes a speedier alternative.

Robert Heinlein said it best: TANSTAAFL; there ain't no such thing as a free lunch. As we have seen here, most financial institutions will charge you at least once, and sometimes twice or three times, to shift your money from point A to point B. Even FirePay and NETeller, which are free services as of this writing, aren't in it for their health. They hold a lot of people's money for a short or a long period of time, and while they're holding on to it, they enjoy the "float"; they can invest it as they see fit, and reap the return. Like the man said, TANSTAAFL.

PROMOTIONS AND BONUSES

While it's true that there's no such thing as a free lunch, you can enjoy a cost-free snack from time to time. One such time is when you're making your first deposit to an online poker site, because many sites sweeten the pot at that time by offering cash bonuses to first-time players. These bonuses may be anything from a waived tournament fee to a flat payment or a percentage bonus scaled to the size of your deposit. I hesitate to name specific sites and deals, because offers are, as we know, subject to change without notice, but a common add-on would be 25 percent on top of your initial deposit, up to a limit such as $50.

Better than a sharp stick in the eye.

With so many online sites to choose from, and so many sites vying for your business, it only makes sense to shop around and skim a little extra from each. Over time you'll decide where you like to play based on the functionality and reliability of the site, the types of games they offer, look-and-feel issues, and the quality of the competition. Until that time, it makes sense to sample, and it especially makes sense to sample the sites that offer you free money for doing so. You might compare this with small-town cardrooms that offer $40-for-$20 bonuses to first-time players. They have to do something to attract new business, and their promotional outlay is your gain. Go ahead and grab that bonus.

At the same time, don't get carried away. Just because you got an extra double-sawbuck from www.flopheadsgalore.com, that's no reason to go nuts at the site and play sloppy poker. Don't pretend you're playing with the house's money; once they shift it into your account, it's *yours*, and you should treat it accordingly. Likewise, just because a site offers a sliding scale of bonuses—*Deposit more and we'll give you more!*—that's no reason for you to move off your solid money management techniques. Deposit only what *you* feel comfortable depositing. Don't let the promise of free money turn your head.

Some sites also offer bonuses to players who sign up their friends. If you have friends who are interested, and you've found a site you like, by all means avail yourself of these bonuses. But do yourself a favor and restrict your recruiting efforts to your own friends. Many is the sad sack who decided he could get rich by casting spam far and wide across the Internet, inviting staggering numbers of strangers to be his friend for the purpose of reaping this bonus. Regular readers of rec.gambling.poker recognize this ploy for what it is: annoying noise that must be shouted down.

Some sites offer freeroll tournaments with cash prize pools funded by the house. These are a tremendously good deal on a couple of levels. First, of course, they're free, so the risk-reward ratio is, well, infinite. Second, they offer the opportunity to see a lot of cards and play a lot of hands. For someone new to a site, or new to a certain form of poker, or even new to poker altogether, this is an ideal opportunity to get in a lot of learning for a zero dollar investment. Suppose you've played a lot of hold'em but never tried your hand at Omaha/8. You could do your learning on the free-play side, but as we've already discussed, while you can learn the structure of the game that way, you'll learn very little about effective strategy. Playing in a freeroll tournament gives you the best of both worlds: it costs nothing to enter, but the fact that there's real money at stake means that your opponents will play a serious game of poker, and you can go to school on that.

So shop the sites for freerolls, add-ons, promotions, and bonuses of every stripe. By using these offers effectively, you can enhance your bankroll and extend your online play with little or no cost to you. Just remember not to let the tail wag the dog. A $10 discount does you no good if it puts you into a game or a limit that's not right for you. Also be wary of bonuses tied to hours of play. For the sake of collecting a $25 bonus, you could end up having to spend hours and hours in a totally unfavorable game situation, losing far more than the bonus lets you gain.

THE RAKE

Just how much money does it cost to play online? How much does the house take per hand, and how does that number affect your play?

If you're a low-limit player, in the $1–$2 range, you'll find that the maximum rake is about a dollar a hand, and then only if the pot is above a certain size. At the higher limits, $10–$20 and above, rakes top out around $3 per hand, depending on the pot size. Though that might not seem like much—a dollar here, a dollar there—before you know it, the house is pulling down $30, $40, $50 a table and more. Good for them. The house has to make a profit, or else it couldn't host the game, leaving the rest of us cast adrift in a pokerless wasteland.

But count on this: the rake will be higher, per hour of play, on the Internet than it will be in a b&m cardroom. If you think you know the reason, write it here.

_____

_____

That's right: more hands per hour; therefore more pots; therefore more rake. A b&m cardroom might pull a dollar a pot out of 20 to 30 hands an hour. An Internet site can easily deal twice that many hands and more. True, a certain percentage of those hands will be at shorthanded tables, and though the rake at a shorthanded table is proportionally smaller than at a full table, it never drops to zero, so the house is drawing down *something* on almost every flop, whether there are two players going at it or ten.

The impact of this is easiest to see in head-to-head competition. Suppose you and your foe faced each other down with $100 each at a $1–$2 limit table. While many sites, like many cardrooms, have a no-flop, no-drop policy, unless you and your adversary are planning to fold blinds till kingdom comes, eventually you're going to see some flops, and each flop will cost you a minimum of $.25. Suppose the two of you are evenly matched; you could expect to play each other to a draw over the course of 500 hands. How much money would you each actually have after that time? Considering only the smallest possible rake, $.25, after 500 flops the house will have collected $125! You and your foe will *both* be down $62.50!

How do you like them (expensive) apples?

I give you this one-on-one example to demonstrate the grim inevitable drain that the rake represents on your stack. One-on-one play against an equally skilled opponent is, to twist the phrase, a license to lose money. At the same time, heads-up online poker will turn out to be one of your most profitable situations. Why? Because there are times when you'll find yourself absolutely dominating an opponent. In those situations it's not a question of *whether* you will win, but rather *how much* and *how fast*. The faster you take his money, the less onerous the rake will be.

At a full, ten-handed table, ten players share the burden of the rake, so the impact on each individual player is correspondingly less. In this situation, you can afford to play patiently, just as you would in a b&m. But, just as in a b&m, the rake never goes away. Hand after hand, flop after flop, hour after hour, day after day, the rake eats into your bankroll. If you expect to be a net-plus player on the Internet (or anywhere in the public poker realm) you have to overcome not just your foes, but your foes *plus* the rake. It's a big hill to climb, a hidden cost of playing poker that, in and of itself, explains why so many otherwise skillful players can't make a living at the game.

Knowledgeable players will, at this point, point out the obvious: *Yeah, but at least there's no dealer to tip*. True, very true. In a b&m cardroom, you can expect to tip the dealer a buck or two on every hand you win. If you win five hands an hour, that's $5 an hour out of your win rate, another ridge on the hill of poker you have to climb. So in this sense, online poker is a better bargain than the real-world game. *But only in this sense*. You still have to overcome the rake, and the rake is still going to be higher because they're dealing more hands. Of course, your win rate should be higher, too, assuming you're a winning player, because you'll be seeing a lot more situations where your skill makes you a favorite over your foes.

The rake is a delicate matter for any cardroom, in cyberspace or anyplace. If the rake is too high, it grinds the players down to poverty and kills the game completely. If the rake is too low, the house can't make enough money to stay in business. And always the house is looking over at what the competition is up to. Far be it from me to suggest price fixing, but you won't find much variation in rake in any closed poker environment. Casinos in Las Vegas all charge about the same; the collection fees in Southern California cardrooms never vary much from one to the next. Likewise in cyberspace. They all charge about the same. You might argue that they all charge too much, and I might agree, but it's their game and their rules.

If you don't like the rake rate, there are two things you can do. First, complain. Send an e-mail to technical support and tell them you think they're charging too much. It might make no difference, but it doesn't hurt to try. Second, play at the highest limit for a given rate structure. A $2–$4 and a $5–$10 table, for example, might very well take the same maximum of $3 out of any pot of $60 or more. At $5–$10, that maximum will be reached much more frequently (it may never be reached at $2–$4) and any money above $60 that goes into the pot is, essentially, rake-free. In all cases, you minimize the impact of the rake by seeking the highest ratio between rake and bet size. A $2 rake at a $10–$20 table represents a rake that's 10 percent the size of the big bet. A $1 rake at a $2–$4 table represents a rake that's 25 percent the size of a big bet. You'll do much better in the long run with the $2 rake because the proportional cost is so much less.

Some sites, especially new sites in the hunt for new cus-

tomers, discount their rake and loudly proclaim this fact—
lowest rake on the Internet!—in their ads and promotions. All
other things being equal, you might as well go to a site
with a substantially lower rake than its competitors. Just remember that all other things may not be equal. They may
not, for example, have a sufficiently large player base to
offer you a profitable game situation no matter how low
the rake. Or their software may be so kludgy that what you
gain in reduced rake you lose right back in frustration-
induced tilt.

Still, occasionally all other things *are* equal, and then
rake surfing becomes a target of opportunity for the savvy
online poker player. How do you exploit the opportunity?
By scouring each online poker room's website for rake information. They all post it, though sometimes you have to
search around to find it. When you do, it can become part
of the database you build in deciding where to play. Just as
you would seek to exploit the discounts and bonuses that
the site offers, you should try to glean every edge over the
rake that you possibly can. They're small edges, one and
all, but small edges do add up.

CASHING OUT

There comes a time when you want to take your money off
the table. At the b&ms this is easy. You just rack your chips,
haul them to the cage, convert them into cash, put the cash
in your wallet, and trundle on back home. Online, this proposition is not so simple. Oh, the matter of requesting a pay-
out is easy enough. Just go to the cashier and jump through
the requisite elementary hoops, and your money will be
winging its way back to FirePay or your credit card, or com-

ing to you via check, in a matter of cyber moments. What's not so simple is the state of mind you might find yourself in when you go to make this move.

Let's say you started out playing on www.drawingdead. com with an online bankroll of $500 in real money. You spent time in the free-play area, then jumped over to the real-money tables and found a comfortable home at the $3–$6 level—not a bad place to play with a $500 bankroll backing your action. You've been running well. Through a combination of fortitude, concentration, and discipline, you've doubled your $500 stake and are now carrying around $1,000 in your electronic pocket. At this moment you encounter a common quandary of online poker: Should you or should you not take profit?

Part of you wants to. You're $500 ahead. You could withdraw that $500 and continue to play on the site with, essentially, house money for as long as you like. Or no, not as long as you like; rather, as long as you last. Suppose you start running bad? Suppose you turn that remaining $500 into an even zero? Then you'll have to go through the hassle (and possible expense) of reloading your online poker gun. This won't make you happy, nor should it; everyone hates the rebuy. So maybe you'll just leave that extra $500 where it is, as insurance against a losing streak.

In this example we see the difference between a real-world bankroll and its online equivalent. In the real world, you can pull your money out of the game and put it back in with absolute ease. You can draw profits from your bankroll any time you like for as much or as little as you like, tapping it for anything from a cup of coffee to a Lexus. The consequences of taking too much are minimized because you can easily replenish your bankroll from other resources. Online, though, the division between your bankroll and the rest of your assets is so clear and extreme . . .

it's as if there's a wall between the two sets of funds. For the sake of not having to climb that wall back and forth, paying for it every time you do, you might very well just leave all of your bankroll right where it is.

And that's not even considering the possibility that you might want to step up. Again, suppose you've turned $500 into $1,000. The logic of poker tells you that if you're a net-plus player, you'll make more money playing for higher stakes. It's not so simple as that, of course—you will encounter more skillful players at higher limits. But for the sake of this discussion, let's assume that your win rate would be one big bet per hour whether you were playing $3–$6 or $5–$10. Obviously, you'd make more money putting in your hours at $5–$10. Just as obviously, your bankroll swings will be bigger at the higher limits. While a $500 bankroll might survive those swings at $3–$6, it's at much greater risk—to the point of being foolishly imperiled—at $5–$10.

So your plan to move up, or even the unfocused prospect that someday you *might* move up, augers against withdrawing any of your hard-won profit. And here we have a classic trap of online poker: some people never, ever cash out. They leave their cybercash, original bankroll and profit alike, in play on the Internet poker site until some big negative fluctuation sadly brings them down to zero. Then they either rebuy or stop playing, in either case never having enjoyed any tangible gain from their gain.

It's something like the art collector who buys a lot of paintings as investments. She watches them appreciate in value but also falls in love with them, so that somehow she can never bring herself to sell them. Then one day they're destroyed in a fire, and she ends up with neither the paintings nor the profit. There's a saying among collectors: *You don't own things; things own you.* The same might be said of your online bankroll. If you never take profit, your profit never exists.

But this reluctance to take profit is almost Newtonian in its perfect inertia—so much so that we can cast it as a law of motion, thus: *Money online tends to stay online unless acted upon by an outside force.* That outside force is you, making the decision to take some of your money off the virtual felt. While I'm all for building a bankroll, I'm also a realist. Sooner or later, we all run bad. If you run your account down to zero, you will have gotten nothing from your hours of online play except, well, hours of online play. Though that's not nothing, it's also not a Lexus, nor even a cup of coffee.

Some people don't see it this way. They reckon that the benefit of winning is *it lets you stay in action.* They reason that being able to play for as long as they want, and as high as they want, is sufficient profit from their profit. If that's how you see it, you won't get a strenuous argument from me.

May I suggest a compromise?

It's a given that you don't want to stunt your bankroll to the point where you risk going broke and can never move up. It's also a given that you'd like to see at least some real-world gain from your labors. Given these givens, why not employ the *double/half rule*?

The double/half rule proposes that every time you double your online bankroll, you cash out half your profit. If you start out with $1,000 and run it up to $2,000, you cash out $500—half your profit—and leave the other $1,500 where it is. When you double through again, turning $1,500 into $3,000, you draw down $750, and so on. In this way, you get to maintain a substantial and growing bankroll while at the same time reaping some non-poker benefit from your play.

This formula makes a couple of assumptions. First, it assumes that you're going to be a winning player, confronted with the happy problem of what to do with all that profit. Second, it assumes that your interest lies in maintaining an online poker presence without going all out in search of big-time poker profit. If you still cling to the notion that online poker is to be your career, I'll remind you again that a lamentably small number of wannabe professional poker players ever realize that goal in any poker venue, real-world or virtual. And the online version has its own special hazards. Still, some people can't resist jumping into deep water, whether they've checked for rocks or not.

BUYING A BANKROLL

If you're one of the industrious few who have decided to try making online poker a major revenue stream, then your approach to managing your bankroll will be quite different—and different yet again from the approach you'd take in the b&m realm.

In a cardroom or casino, any player can immediately play as big as his bankroll allows. Cash in your U.S. Savings Bonds to the tune of 25 grand, say, and you'll be welcome to a seat in any game in town. If you lose that money, you can go into your pocket for more, and keep going into your pocket at will until your pocket or your will run dry.

Online, by contrast, you'll find strict limits to the amount of bankroll you can build and the pace at which you can put it together. These limits exist to protect both the player and the house.

The sites know that if they didn't impose buy-in limits, certain disreputable types would victimize them through, for example, credit card fraud. Here's how that would work (kids, don't try this at home): Let's say you can plunk ten grand all at once into a game, charging it to your credit card, which, for the sake of this example, also places no constraints on the transaction. You jump into the game, play very badly, and lose all your money. Actually, you lose on purpose, dumping your chips off to a confederate who then cashes out just as quickly as he can. You, meanwhile, now call your credit card company and tell them to put a stop on your payment. You never meant to bet that big, you say; you were seduced by the site and you don't want to honor your debt. Now the online site is involved in a whole big dispute with your credit card company, a dispute in which it has the natural legal disadvantage of being not just a gaming enterprise but an offshore one at that. To prevent this sort of scam, and a whole host of related ones, all online sites limit the amount of cyberchips any player can buy at one time.

Buy-in limits protect the player, too, at least according to the online sites. They worry that, without these limits, compulsive gamblers would go nuts online and get into a vicious cycle of *lose, rebuy, lose, rebuy, lose, rebuy, lose* until fatigue and remorse set in, and the hapless bettor severs his connection with the online site, or possibly his wrists. To keep players from going down too far too fast (and exposing themselves to the legal or financial risk of having abetted this) the online sites put strict buy-in limits in place.

And what are these limits? They vary somewhat from site to site, but these figures are typical as of this writing:

- $600 per 24-hour period
- $1,500 per 7-day period
- $2,000 per 30-day period

Limits are somewhat higher if you're making a deposit via wire transfer or cashier's check for the manifest reason that middlemen—and potential rancorous disputes with same—are absent from these transactions. Also, once you've established a track record on most sites you can ask for and receive a loosening of your limits.

Which you're definitely going to need if you plan to play big online.

Suppose it's your goal to rip 'em up at the $20–$40 limit. Using the *hundred-to-one thumbnail* (which suggests that an adequate bankroll for a given limit is one hundred times the big bet at that limit), you'd want a $4,000 bankroll to play that game comfortably on a regular basis. You'll have to wait until your second 30-day period before you'll be able to put that kind of money in play. So what do you do in the meantime? Play smaller—much smaller—and nurse your bankroll. Maybe don't even play at all, for you certainly don't want to get into a situation in which you're supposed to be building a bankroll but careless play at lower limits has turned your first month's $2,000 bankroll into, say, $580. At that point, when 30 days have passed and you add another two grand to your stack, you still won't have a big enough bankroll to play correctly at your chosen limit. You'll be playing with scared money on a short bankroll—a recipe for disaster in any poker game anywhere.

This vexing problem of buy-in limits tries the patience of many players. Having committed themselves to playing big on the Internet, they certainly don't want to waste a month or two waiting for that to happen. But if they don't take the time to build an appropriate bankroll, they can't expect to play optimally, and their win-rate will suffer. There is simply no alternative to going slowly, playing small (or not at all), and building your bankroll by degrees.

This isn't necessarily a bad thing. Given that you're not likely to play your best online game at first, it's actually a blessing that you can't play big from day one. And why are you not likely to play your best game at first? For one thing, you're playing with virtual chips, which won't seem like real money at first. Until you learn to treat virtual chips as you would treat real cash money, you're likely to play too loose online. (You'll be in good company. Almost everyone plays too loose at first.) So even if it's your plan to play big and win big, be content to start small and go slow. Allow yourself to let your skill set and your bankroll grow together until both are large enough to dominate the game.

PUTTING YOUR CHIPS IN PLAY

Once you have a bankroll adequate to your chosen limit, and abilities equal to the task, you're ready to put your chips in play. A logical question to ask at this point would be, "Well, how much should I put in play?" The answer is not quite the same as it would be in a b&m game.

In most poker situations it makes good strategic sense to be the big stack at the table. One strategy that serves this purpose is to figure out what a typical buy-in is, and then buy in for twice that amount. This has the effect of making you look like a big gun from the start. It's an especially useful piece of misdirection to direct against players joining the game after you do. If you're playing $3–$6, for example, and most people buy in for $100, you buy in for $200. Then when new players join the game, they will draw a couple of false conclusions, first assuming that you bought in for $100 like everyone else, and second that you've already doubled through. This strategy has limits to its utility in real-world games, where the lineup of players can remain unchanged for several hours, and where attentive players will remember that you bought in large at the start.

But the online environment is much more dynamic. Players come and go quickly, and it doesn't take long for the whole lineup of a table to roll over. Soon there won't be anyone sitting there who knows what you bought in for, and then your big stack will be the psychological and strategic weapon you want it to be.

By that logic, then, why not just bring your whole bankroll with you when you come? Suppose you have 1,000 virtual dollars squirreled away on a site. Why not buy in to that $3–$6 game for the full one grand? That would give you a totally dominating image, wouldn't it?

Well, yes it might, but there are two very good reasons why you never want to put your whole bankroll into play online. The first is just one of good money management. Suppose you went on horrible tilt, the kind of watching-a-train-wreck tilt that you see happening but just can't escape. In the worst case, you might go through your whole online bankroll and put yourself out of action in one disastrous session. You can easily protect yourself by simply holding some of your bankroll back. This way if you do go on tilt, and want to *keep* going on tilt, you'll at least have to leave the table long enough to get more chips—long enough, hopefully, to come to your senses.

More important, give consideration to the matter of changing tables. You might be playing in a fair-to-middling $3–$6 game, while vigilantly scanning the sign-up board for better opportunities elsewhere. When one comes up, if you have some bankroll in reserve, you can grab that other seat right away, without having to leave the game you're in and running the risk that the seat you want may have been snatched up by someone else. If all of your money is in play at table A, you'll have to cash out completely before moving to table B. Through this process, a real strategic opportunity may very well be lost.

So you want to buy in for enough money that you can be a dominating force at your limit, but you don't want to put your whole bankroll at risk or commit all your chips to one game at the expense of lucrative alternatives. This reasoning underscores the absolute need to pick the right limit for your bankroll. You never want to be short money at any table, but you also never want to over-commit your bankroll. Pick a limit that will let you buy in big with no more than one-third of your bankroll. In this way, you'll have another one-third to buy in to another game, while still holding a third of your bankroll in reserve against disaster. Online poker is not entirely a closed financial environment. You *can* put more money in, but it's not easy, and it should be avoided unless you're trying to buy your bankroll up to a certain size. With that in mind, you'll generally want to play smaller, relative to the size of your bankroll, than you might in a b&m environment, where rebuilding your bankroll requires nothing more than a brisk walk to the ATM.

If you're out of money, you're out of action, so protecting your bankroll should be your prime directive. Of course no one wants to lose and no one expects to lose. But losses do happen. Big losses can be catastrophic to limited bankrolls, and your online bankrolls will generally, of necessity, be more limited than their real-world equivalents. If you're playing at the appropriate limit with the right number of chips, you can weather the storms.

But if you're in over your head, you drown.

4

♣ ♠ ♦ ♥

MOOD MANAGEMENT

Keeping a rein on your emotions is important to successful play in any poker game. Let your feelings rule your play and you can find yourself making counter-productive, even self-destructive moves at the table. A conscientious and self-aware poker player constantly monitors his inner weather. This sort of player knows that managing one's mood is more than just a matter of not going on tilt or not playing when you're tired, stoned, or stupid. It's hard enough to maintain this sort of emotional equilibrium in a real-world game, but as you shall see, the online poker environment provides its own special challenges to a player's attempt to keep an even keel.

THE POKER FACE IN PRIVATE

When a certain sort of player takes a bad beat, he experiences *psychic pain,* and reacts in a certain way. In the moment he feels that pain, making the pain go away becomes his most important concern. He's no longer interested in playing perfect poker, but only in feeling less bad about himself and his current circumstances. In the b&ms, these players take certain typical steps to ease their psychic pain. They throw cards at the dealer, criticize their fellow players' play, or try to get the player sitting next to them to concur that their luck is miserable and the universe is unfair. Each of these outbursts represents two definite leaks in a player's game. First, it reveals a player who's thinking about the wrong thing; second, it shows everyone a player less concerned with playing well than feeling well—always an easy target for a smart player's attack. These outbursts are always counterproductive in the sense that they're big, fat tells, but they can have the effect of settling a player down. At least he gets it out of his system.

When bad outcomes strike the online poker player, though, he experiences them in isolation. He feels as though he has been victimized by his foes' stupidity or the poker gods' cold injustice, *and he has nowhere to vent his feelings!* There are no cards to throw, no dealers to curse, no friends at other tables on whom to vent his spleen. He may opt to type something tart in the chat window—"how could u play that cheez?"—but it's hardly the same sensation as a good, hearty, real-world rant. He could even *yell* at the screen, but you know what they say, "In cyberspace, no one can hear you scream."

You could argue that these victim reactions have no place in a sensible poker player's game, and I could hardly agree with you more. But the fact is that we're not always the sensible poker players we would wish ourselves to be, and when we experience bad outcomes, we do, in some sense, have to get it out of our systems. The b&m environment, by the mere fact of it being a total poker environment, offers relief from these feelings in a way that the online environment does not.

If you play online, then, you need to be prepared to experience all of your emotions in isolation. When bad beats happen, they happen to you alone. No one else will share your pain. Because of this solo voyage through misery, a bad beat is much more likely to put you on tilt online. Wait, it gets worse. Not only do you not have your normal means of venting frustration, you also have to deal with the accelerated pace of play. If you should happen to go on tilt, even for a few moments, you'll see quite a few more hands than you would in a b&m, and have quite a few more opportunities to make tilty, irrational decisions based not on good poker play but upon your need to get well quick and relieve your psychic pain.

It's the old familiar rationalization. You get A-A snapped by 8-2 offsuit, and decide, well, if that's the way it's going to be, you'll play 8-2 offsuit too. In the real-world, you'll have a moment between hands to come to your senses. On the Internet, that decision is made before you've had a chance to recover from the beat that inspired it.

Not all players experience bad beats this way. Not all players go on tilt. Those who have a natural predisposition toward tranquility will do fine online, just as they do in the real world. Those prone to tilt will suffer more. So, again, you have to ask yourself honestly what kind of player you are. If you're a hothead, you may find that the online environment is a pressure cooker in which you will, quite literally, stew in your own juices.

Think about the worst experience of tilt you've ever had. What triggered it, and how did you respond? How do you think your experience would be different if you had been playing online at the time?

_____

_____

Expanding this discussion slightly, we can see that all of our poker emotions take place in a vacuum online. We experience not just our failures but also our triumphs—*I bluffed you, sucker!*—alone. Sitting by yourself, staring at a computer screen, there's really no reason for you to keep a lid on your feelings, no percentage in maintaining a poker face. In the course of an online session, you might find yourself talking out loud to that screen or arguing with it or laughing at it. Playing online, you can give voice to a whole range of feelings that, for strategic reasons or to avoid embarrassment, you would never dare to show in a real-world game.

As a result of this freedom to express, we find that we experience our own emotions more intensely. And they get inside our heads. This sounds strange, I know. Since the feelings *start out* in our heads, how can they *get inside* our heads? They do so by coloring the way we approach our play. Our feelings literally infect our logical process, and if we don't take care to inoculate ourselves against this inner virus, it can spread with disastrous effect.

The Buddhist concept of "right action, right mind" comes into play here. In a real-world game, the right thing to do is to mute your reactions, lest you give away information to your foes. As a consequence, you temper your feelings as well. The right action or behavior leads to the right mind or feeling. Like a good relief pitcher in baseball, you feel neither great elation nor grand depression; you just do your job. That's in the real world, when you're in the zone.

Online, though, you can let it all hang out, all the time, every hand. When your flush card hits the board, you pump your fist and say, "Yes!" When you're running a bluff, you illogically help your opponent lay down his hand by chanting, "Fold, fold, fold, fold, fold." It seems that there's no harm in this. It seems that you're just using the peculiar isolated nature of online play to express what you don't get to express in a real-world game. Obviously you don't want to carry this kind of broad expressiveness back into a b&m game, and logically you would not. That isn't the risk. The risk is that you'll let the broad expressiveness affect your decision making. You'll remember how you ran a bluff, chanted "Fold, fold, fold," and got the other fellow to lay down. You'll remember—and you'll do it again, whether the situation warrants this decision or not.

There's a lot of verbal "what-the-hell-ism" when you're playing online. You're dealt 9-4 offsuit, but you're in late position and no one has raised, so you say, "What the hell," and click *call*. Or maybe you even raise. *What the hell?* The fact of not having to control your expressions can make you lose control of your decisions.

I'm not saying that every player will experience online play this way. I'm just saying that it can happen, and it might happen to you without your even knowing it.

As a test of your own reactions, next time you play online make a record of everything you say out loud. Correlate it if you can to circumstances where you veer away from optimum decision making.

What you think of as a luxury of online play—you can say what you want in the privacy of your own home—may turn out to be a startling leak in your game.

THE PROBLEM WITH THE VIRTUAL CHIPS

The problem with virtual chips is that they're just that— virtual. They don't exist in any meaningful sense except as a number on your screen, a series of digits there by your virtual chair or the avatar that represents your play. Watching those digits rise or fall is in no way the same experience as watching your chip stack wax and wane. The difference—the distance, if you will, between money and chips—can have a negative impact on your play.

In the real world, when you sit down to play, you make an exchange. You take cash money out of your pocket or wallet, and hand it to a dealer or chip runner who converts your money into chips. You see the change take place, and while you're at the table, you're acutely aware of the relationship between money and chips. The chips don't just represent money—they *are* money. You accord them with respect, and make your decisions based at least partly on that respect. You value your chips, in other words, because you draw a close connection between those chips and spendable green.

Online, that connection is more abstract. The "money" you're playing with right now has made a journey from your wallet to your bank account and thence to the site via FirePay or some other route. Now you've taken an arbitrary number of betting units out of your online account and attached them to your place at the table. It's easy to view that number as a mere number and forget that it's money at all.

Many online players, especially those new to the experience, will therefore have trouble exercising proper poker discipline. They'll call too liberally and chase too much. And while I urge every new player to spend time at the free-play tables, it's worth noting that the numbers representing chips at the free-play tables look exactly the same as the numbers representing chips in real cash games. On some innate level you can confuse the two, and play in a real-money game as if it were a free-play game. Not good.

What's required, then, is a certain *inner attentiveness* that helps you guard against disconnecting your online chips from the real-money value they represent. It's just a number on the screen *at this moment,* but one day it will be a dollar in your pocket once again. Remember the dollar that it was, and the dollar it will be, and you're less likely to be careless with it in its temporary, transitory, virtual form.

Why is this a mood issue and not a strategy issue? Because at this moment your relationship with that virtual dollar is not a strategic one but an emotional one. If you allow yourself to feel online money differently from the way you feel real money, you will play differently. Probably you'll play too loose. Possibly you will also play with less focus and concentration, because you'll discount the amount your decisions matter.

On the other side of the (literal, metaphorical, or virtual) coin, wise poker didacts routinely counsel players not to take the money too seriously. They point out, and rightly so, that a player too keenly focused on the dollar value of his chips may make poor decisions out of fear—the fear of losing the very value those chips represent. I'm certainly not counseling you to play scared, but I think the risk of this is much less than its opposite. Again, because your virtual money is so many transactions and conversions removed from cash money in your pocket, you're much more likely to play careless than to play scared.

Unless you're near the bottom of your bankroll. As I've already pointed out, for most online players, the name of the game should be *don't rebuy*. By nursing your bankroll and playing at limits appropriate to your bankroll, you can make online poker an open-ended and self-sustaining activity . . . you can play for years on your initial buy-in if you do it right. But if you're running bad and on the verge of running out, then you will start running scared. You'll depart from optimum performance, play too tight, and suffer the consequences accordingly. If you reach this point, where your bankroll is imperiled and it's affecting your play, then you must drop down to low limits, or even micro limits, and set out to rebuild your stack slowly and patiently. You don't have to get well in a hurry. All you have to do is not die.

In real-world games, there's a concept known as *racking off*. A player who's approaching the end of his rack, especially one who has decided to quit if/when his rack runs out, will start to play very badly as his chips become few. He will have decided that there's not much difference between losing 85 betting units and losing 100, and so he'll pee away the last 15, or 1,500, dollars as if they didn't count somehow. This is emotionally self-indulgent behavior, but in the b&m realm it's not totally disastrous, because the player can easily get back in action. Online, given the hassle and expense of moving money into play, racking off is something to be avoided at all cost. You can accomplish this by never forgetting that your virtual money is real money—just currently in a different form—and that a dollar won is a dollar won, whether it's the first or the last one left in your rack.

As a point of information, some sites, such as www.truepoker.com, represent your table stake as stacks of chips, not numbers on the screen. This can be helpful not just in reminding yourself that the stakes are real but also in keeping an eye on your opponents' holdings. The screen representation of chips much more closely resembles players' holdings in a real cardroom or casino. It's a small thing, but success in online poker depends on the accumulation of many small things done right. If looking at a stack of virtual chips is more helpful to you than looking at a set of digits on a screen, pick a site that displays players' money in this way.

THE MANIAC FEEDBACK LOOP

Maniacs are a common poker player's complaint. Those who play a sensible game are often frustrated, thwarted, or just generally vexed by players who figure, "They can't figure out your strategy if you don't have one." On some level we know that these trashmeisters are their own worst enemies. Give them enough time and they will impale themselves on the bayonet of their own bad play. Trouble is, we may be part of the shish kebab too. Playing against maniacs requires its own special set of strategy and tactics.

In cardrooms and casinos, you're not likely to find more than one or two maniacs at any given table. Online, though, you'll encounter many more maniacs—so many that it often seems as if whole tables have taken leave of their senses. Why should this be? I can think of three reasons. How many can you think of? You go first.

_____

_____

Okay, here's mine.

First, a number of online poker players legitimately don't know what they're doing. They may be judged maniacs by default, but the fact is that they're just basically clueless. Remember that for many players, online poker is their first public poker experience. They wouldn't be caught dead in a b&m, couldn't face the embarrassment of being thus exposed in their innocence and ignorance. But the anonymity of online play lures a lot of first-timers into action, where their ineptitude can wreak collateral damage on those nearby.

Second, online players are not accountable for their actions. A lot of players would like to be maniacs, but can't sell that image in the b&ms. They're too shy or scared to play ultra-aggressively if they know that people will be watching, criticizing, and condemning them directly for their maniacal play. Online, the cloak of anonymity allows wannabe maniacs to hide behind their avatars, and play a much more wide-open game than they can ever manage in the real world.

Third, as we've already seen, online it's easy to lose track of the fact that the money you're playing for is real. If your table has several people suffering from this value-disconnect, suddenly it's a play-money table. Starting requirements and common sense go out the window. Raising wars break out. Pots get capped. Multi-way action is the norm. And the hands that win—*whoo, boy, stinky cheese!*

It's this last fact, the fact of bad hands winning big pots, that ultimately triggers the maniac feedback loop. If you're an otherwise sensible player, but you see people dragging monster pots with 9-4 offsuit, you'll find yourself sorely tempted to dive in. Pretty soon it's all aboard for wacky-land. Add to this the accelerated pace of online play, and you have a recipe for genuine frenzy. A table reaches critical mass of madness and detonates into nonstop nonsense: the maniac feedback loop.

How do you beat a table full of online maniacs? The same way you beat b&m maniacs. Tighten up your calling requirements, bluff infrequently, and press your edges aggressively. Recognize that in this environment you will experience big fluctuations, and plan to roll with those punches. When mostly everyone is playing garbage, mostly garbage is going to win. Though it can be profitable to play with maniacs, it's vital that you not sink to their level. Cling to your calling requirements. Don't lose your head, even when headlessness seems to be both the norm and the winning strategy.

To cite one example, a typical nose-open online hold'em

game will play well below the any-ace line, which is to say that most players will play any ace with any kicker from any position. If you can maintain your restraint, and throw away your bad aces while those around you are playing theirs, you'll definitely profit from the times when your good aces dominate.

But again, this is not so much a matter of tactics as it is of outlook. The maniac feedback loop sucks players in. Forget strategic considerations and recognize that your entire emotional state is at stake. Play among the maniacs, sure; encourage maniacal behavior, by all means; emulate maniac activity when it serves your image; but don't let the maniac's perspective invade your head and heart.

And don't imagine that you're immune from the same temptations. The anonymity that protects newbies and crazies protects you as well. When you know you're just an avatar to your foes, you can find yourself rationalizing all sorts of strangeness. The feeling that the money's not real might cause others to make loose, chasey calls; it could have the same effect on you. And your own isolation can breed within you a certain sense of cabin fever, inspiring delusions and mistakes. The online environment is deceptively challenging; your guard must never come down.

RESENTMENT

Most poker players experience resentment from time to time, directed mostly at lucky players and at bullies. We resent the lucky player just for *being* lucky, for stealing chips and pots that we somehow regard as "rightfully ours." We resent the poker bully not just for pushing us around, but also for having the moxie to do so. In the b&m's, we keep our resentments in check because we know that revealing them to other players hurts our strategic goals in the game. Online, as we've seen, there's no penalty for giving voice to our feelings. We can be as loud as we want to with our resentments. But the louder we are with our resentments, the more deeply we feel them. They may ultimately overwhelm us, to the point where we're playing poker not to win money, or even to have fun, but merely for *revenge*.

It's fairly common, for example, for an unsuspecting player to find himself tangling with an online bully. If this happens in a shorthanded or one-on-one situation, the bully can end up punishing his victim and taking a lot of money. You would expect this experience to breed within the victim a healthy respect for the bully and an aversion to mixing it up with that guy. Curiously, the opposite often proves true. Having been pushed around by a bully, many players actually seek out the opportunity to take on the bully again. They want to get even—not financially even, but psychologically even. "You pushed me around last time, so this time I'm going to push you right back!"

In case you've forgotten or never heard the first law of Killer Poker, here it is again:

> *Don't challenge strong players.*
> *Challenge weak ones.*
> *That's what they're there for.*

If you have a desire to get even, financially even, go find some inferior foe who will accommodate that urge. If you have a desire to get emotionally even, dismiss it. It's irrelevant at best and counterproductive at worst.

On the other hand, if someone has gotten lucky at your expense, by all means track them down and tackle them again. If they truly had to get lucky to beat you, then in the long run you will make money by engaging them in play.

Note, though, that you're going after them for sound strategic reasons, and not just to make yourself feel good.

This business of wanting to make yourself feel good has an incredible potency in the online environment. Because you're playing with no human contact except the pro forma responses of your action buttons and the minimal communication of your chat box, it's easy to develop imagined or phantom adversarial relationships with your foes. You can't see them or hear them; in a fundamental sense you can't know them. You end up filling in the blanks. You paint pictures of your opponents based solely on their actions, and you respond emotionally to these artificial constructs.

Not just emotionally but *very* emotionally. You have these intense one-way relationships with other players, relationships that are fundamentally unsatisfying because they *are* one way. The risk here is obvious. You end up playing not according to the situation but according to the way you feel about your foes.

Example: You come across a player who doesn't seem terribly knowledgeable. He sticks around in the face of your raise, takes an inside straight draw with inferior odds, catches lucky, and wins the pot. Now you not only resent him for getting lucky, you feel vastly superior to him, and you utterly disrespect his ability. He may be worthy of your disrespect and then again he may not, but in any case from this point forward you will objectify him completely in your mind. He's no longer an adversary, he's a *hated enemy*. Your twin feelings of superiority and resentment will, if you're not very careful, dominate the way you play. Emotion, not strategy, becomes the guiding principle of your play.

To understand the full impact of emotion on your play, simply draw up a *feelings log* next time you play online.

This log is nothing more than a list of all the emotions you experience when you play online. You might go through apprehension, elation, eagerness, despair, anger, happiness, fear, fatalism, overconfidence, and paranoia, all in the course of a single session of play. If you think that you're always cool, calm, and collected when you play poker, I encourage you to do this exercise at once. You will be amazed at the complex range of emotions you experience and further amazed at the power and intensity they have in the privacy of your own home.

THE PSYCHOLOGICAL DIFFICULTY OF ABSORBING A LOSS ONLINE

Beyond the emotional challenge of butting heads with a bully online, there's always the possibility that he's just flat-out better than you. You should leave, just sign off or change tables or otherwise remove yourself from the line of fire.

Yet you stay. Why might that be?

It's possible that your opponent is better than you *and you don't know it.* Although he seems to be playing more aggressively than you'd like, you may not think that he is superior in any respect except luck. You may believe that you'd be ahead—*way* ahead—if only you were catching your fair share of cards. This may even be true. But it's also irrelevant. In the sort of slugfest we're contemplating here, the last thing that matters is the cards. Against superior opponents, in situations where you need to catch cards to win, you probably *can't* win, because you're relying on skill *and* luck, while your opponent is relying only on skill.

But that's not even the issue. The issue is motivation. Why are you here? Why are you absorbing punishment in an adverse situation? If you know the game not to be good, the reason may be this: you're afraid of taking the loss.

Let's say you have a cyber-bankroll of $1,200 and find yourself messing around heads-up in a $10–$20 limit game. Before you know it, you've peed away $400—a quarter of your bankroll. The thought of quitting now, having lost 25 percent of your total online equity, may be more than you can bear. So you stick around, hoping to get well. After all, you lost it fast, why can't you win it back fast too?

Can you guess what happens next? Your 25 percent dip turns into a 40 percent or 50 percent dip. What started out as an ugly little hole turned into an ugly big hole, just because you couldn't stand to see yourself lose.

There's an irksome self-fulfilling prophecy to this. You butt heads with a better player, who starts to put you on tilt. Seeing yourself lose, you begin to panic. You open up your play, trying to get well soon. This doesn't work, because your opponent is still better than you. And now that you've opened up your play, he's a *lot* better than you. Now you're playing even worse, for even more money. What kind of madness is this? The kind of madness driven by the fear of admitting defeat.

I'm not saying that this is absolutely true of you, but I am asking you to look at yourself honestly and admit it's true if it is. Are you ashamed of acknowledging that your opponent has your number? Do you believe that if you bow out of the game, someone somewhere will be having a big, fat chortle at your expense? Not true! He'll be silently cursing (and congratulating) you for wriggling off the hook. Good players have contempt for bad players, but only those who stick around! If I'm better than you, and you know it, yet you insist on staying involved with me, I'll just assume you're silly or you don't like money. But if you *leave,* I'll admire your courage.

Let me repeat this, because it sounds so strange: If you leave—if you run away—I'll end up admiring your courage. Yes, it's true. It takes courage to leave a game in the middle of a confrontation. You *are* admitting defeat—and it always takes a certain amount of bravery to admit defeat.

So let's not call it defeat. Let's call it a temporary setback. Let's imagine that this imaginary foe who's pummeling you is not actually, objectively, better than you. He just happens to have the best of you right now. Maybe you're just off your game today. These things happen, and it is no disgrace to admit that you're not playing well enough to take the other guy's money.

But it is a disgrace, a terrible disgrace, to just sit there and take it and take it and take it, hand after hand, hoping that the poker gods will rescue you from your self-inflicted bloodletting. *Don't do it!* If you're beat, beat it! If you know you can't win, *and yet you stick around,* you have no one to blame but your own silly self.

CRAP HAPPENS

Join me in a fantasy. It's not a happy fantasy, but it illustrates the point that, sadly in Internet poker, as in life itself, crap happens.

You're playing in an online tournament, staring down your virtual foes, and feeling pretty frisky because you just flopped a set and turned a full house. Not only that, but with straight and flush possibilities on board, and loose foes contending, you are looking to double or triple your stack, easily putting you in position to win the tournament.

Then . . . you hear a strange sound. It sounds like running water—and so it is: water—lots of water, and all of it running from a split washing machine hose, all the way down in the basement. What will you do?

Why, finish out the hand, of course! Broken hoses can always be repaired, but how often do you get a chance to triple through at a key moment in a tournament? As soon as the hand ends, though, you rush off to combat the wet lurking monster in the cellar. Alas, the problem turns out to swamp you, just as it has swamped the basement. You end up never getting back to the tournament. You're blinded off and finish out of the money.

Needless to say, this doesn't happen in real-world tournaments. If a pipe bursts at a b&m, it's the job of the b&m to fix it. If a phone rings at a b&m, someone else has to answer it. If a dog throws up on the carpet at the b&m, it's not your dog and not your problem. One could argue, I suppose, that the b&m could be subject to robbery, earthquake, or some other sort of human or natural disaster, but these events kill everyone's fun, not just yours. Playing online, as you already know or will soon discover, you often have to deal with all sorts of setbacks that have nothing to do with playing online and that impact no one but you. Not so much the setbacks, but the effects they have on your mood impact your overall success or failure in online play.

Life interferes. Plumbing interferes—also roommates, spouses, children, and friends. These worthy folks don't seem to understand that dinner can wait or helping with homework can wait (or fixing the stupid split hose can wait!). They want your attention, and they want it *now*. They just can't grasp that there's something happening at your computer you can't walk away from now. How can you explain that someone called *Muffdoggy* from somewhere called Cardiff is throwing off all his virtual dollars, and if you don't get them *right now*, someone else will?

Dealing with your own distractions is bad enough, but frequently you have to deal with other players' distractions as well. Occasionally you'll find yourself short-handed online against a lineup including a total monkeyfish, who suddenly quits the game on the flimsy pretext of needing to eat or work or treat a ruptured spleen (like that's your problem!). Next thing you know, the other players have dissolved into the ether and you're sitting there staring at *insufficient ante to start hand*. Sigh. Crap happens.

The blessing of Internet poker is that it's always there when you want it. The curse of Internet poker is that it's never so completely and entirely *there* as its real-world equivalent. When you go to a card club, you can expect the game to last as long as there are players present or waiting. And you can see the end of the game coming. Your own schedule is likewise controlled. You arrive when you arrive, and stay till you go. Online play is different. You can get bumped off your server, called away by your spouse, vexed by power outages, victimized by washing machines—many things.

How will you deal with these setbacks? I offer the following shorthand strategies.

1. *Plan Ahead.* If you know that the demons of distraction (kids, spouse, dog, ghost, whatever) will be home soon, don't commit to any hours-long tournaments that you may not get the chance to complete. You won't play your best. You may even look for an excuse to lose so that you can go on to other things.

2. *Pick Your Spots.* If you know that you're looking at a short session, don't play over your head. Short-term fluctuation being what it is, you might be in the middle of a huge downswing at just the moment when you're forced—

forced—by external circumstance to leave the game. I can understand the appeal of filling in the last ten minutes of your pre-commute morning with a few hands of hold'em, but this is a perfect spot to play small, so that even if the hands don't go your way, you won't feel blue when you have to quit.

3. *Stay Cool.* Pipes burst. Servers crash. Blackouts roll. Often in online poker (indeed as in life) you will find yourself facing the explosive defeat of your expectations. (To see why this explosive defeat of expectation is funny to other people, read my book *The Comic Toolbox: How to Be Funny Even If You're Not.*) How will you respond to these setbacks? The chilly online player takes her reverses in stride. She reboots, redials, refocuses, and all with tranquility and grace. She takes the happening of crap as a mere bad beat, a beat that can truly only defeat her if she lets it get under her skin.

4. *Get Serious.* Some frustrations or setbacks are unavoidable, but others stem from our own unwillingness to treat Internet poker as seriously as we treat our real-world game. When you're playing online poker, that should be all you do, just as it would be in the b&m. I'm not saying that you have to let the gushing hose gush on. But you *can* turn off the phone, set aside the newspaper, close the door, and concentrate on the serious game you're playing. Control what you *can* control, as a function of your desire to play the best game you can for as long as you choose to play. In this way, at least, you'll minimize the impact of avoidable problems—leaving only the unavoidable ones to drive you nuts.

Here's a little exercise. Think about a recent example of crap happening in your (poker) life and describe how you dealt with it.

_____

_____

Next, describe how you'd deal with it differently if you could.

_____

＼_____

Next, next time do it *that* way instead.

FRUSTRATION

"www.playpokeronline.com's server is currently offline."

What?! Well, damn, that's no good! I just got home from work . . . battled stupid traffic for a stupid hour and a half . . . and the only thing that kept me from sideswiping the blowhole in the next lane was the prospect of playing poker when I got home. And now you're telling me I CAN'T?!?! Because the stupid server is offline? What the heck kind of racket is this? I demand satisfaction!

Well. Has that ever happened to you? Have you scheduled for yourself a nice fat little online poker session only to be thwarted by circumstances beyond your control? We talked about how crap happens. Now let's talk about a particular reaction to this sort of event—the natural frustration that abounds when hopes are dashed.

You know the feeling in general, of course. You encounter it many times in many different ways in your life. A promised payment for something fails to come through. The job you were *certain* was yours goes to someone else. Your pocket aces—and the attendant prospect of a big win—get swept away by bottom two pair. Frustration!

Frustration inhabits the intersection of *what you want*

and *what you get instead.* You *want* to play poker online. You *get* a busy signal on your dial-up number instead. You *want* to play mid-limit. You *get* a choice between big-bet and baby poker instead. You *want* to take control of your virtual table with brave raises and bold bets. You *get* a bunch of clueless woodentops who couldn't fold a beach towel, much less that piece of cheese 3-2 offsuit that just took you down for four big bets.

Frustration! What are you gonna do about it?

Here's the worst thing you can do, and you know it: go on tilt. You can let frustration wash over you like some virulent tide, sweeping away all conscious thought and useful self-control. When this happens, you forget that virtual money is real money and start throwing off bets, hoping against vain hope that somehow you can *buy your way out of frustration.* This, of course, won't happen.

Okay, plan B. You can find a different game, or in the case of a server crash, a different online site altogether. This is better than going on tilt—or is it? Defeated expectation has a way of poisoning your mood, and even though you think you've left frustration behind, sometimes you discover that it's been following you around. Sure, you can go play at some other site . . . *if* you already have an account set up. But what if you don't? Then you have to download the software, set up an account, move some money, all that noise . . . and all this time you're *not* doing what you want to *be* doing: playing poker.

Frustration!

By the time you've got that new site dialed in (and come to understand its navigational and functional peculiarities) you've wasted *precious poker time.* That dark impatience that drove you before drives you still. How do you rate your chances of playing Killer Poker now?

May I respectfully suggest plan C? You're not going to

like it, for it involves . . . shudder . . . *not* playing poker. Yes, that's right, you heard right. When circumstances conspire to make it difficult for you to play poker online, just roll with that particular punch and *go do something else*. Read a book. Watch a movie. Talk to the spousy-wousy and the kidderlings. Meditate. Masticate. (That means *chew*, you know, not that other thing.) Go for a big bike ride. Do something, anything . . . but *don't play poker*. Because if you manage to get yourself into action while you're aflame with frustration, you won't play well. You can't. And you know it.

"If you can't love it, don't do it. If you don't love it, you won't do it well." For we who play poker, this means that we must play with serenity, focus, and joy, or just not play at all. True in the b&m's; particularly true in the yeasty hothouse of Internet poker. Play in the right mood, or just give your money away.

I hear your protests. I do, and I feel your pain. You cry out in frustration, *That wasn't supposed to happen! It isn't fair!* Well you know what? I don't recall seeing the words "life is fair" on the contract. Servers *will* crash. Your cat *will* unplug your computer. Your darn kid will fall down and scrape his knee at the *worst possible time*. If you expect everything to go your way all the time—or even most of the time—you're asking for disappointment. Followed by frustration. Followed by horrible tilt and the attendant loss of bankroll.

And it will be nobody's fault but your own.

A British friend of mine likes to say, with a certain self-centered fatalism that I adore, "The universe is there to sort you out." I take this to mean that the challenges of daily life are intended not just to thwart my desire or defeat my expectations, but actually to *test my character*. To put it another way, the truth is revealed under pressure. When you're under pressure, what truth will be revealed? That you can handle adversity (even server crashes) with grace and patience? Or that you freak out at the drop of a dial-up connection because you feel *owed* somehow? I hope for your sake that you can stay cool when things don't go your way, because that happens *a lot* in online poker—the technical reality of the game and the quality of the other players conspire to make it so. Don't take external setbacks and convert them into internal punishment. You won't succeed with that approach. Not in online poker, not in cardroom poker, and not in life.

5

♣ ♠ ♦ ♥

MIND MANAGEMENT

I have talked about the emotional realities of Internet poker and how the nature of the game—specifically its isolation from a "real" poker environment—makes it easier to lose emotional control. This same isolation makes it harder to keep concentration and focus in place. This chapter deals with the issues of concentration and focus, examines some familiar pitfalls, and pursues strategies for keeping our top game in place.

DISTRACTION AND UNDERSTIMULATION

As you have already seen, one big difference between on-line and real-world poker is the way the information comes at you online. Instead of finding yourself in a total poker environment, you find yourself in a nearly total *non-poker* environment, with a narrowly defined window of poker no bigger than the screen of your computer. The immediate challenge to your concentration is clear: How will you keep focused on the actions and activities of that tiny screen when there are so many other sources of visual, audio, and sensory input attacking you on all sides?

Take a moment and contemplate those distractions. Do a thorough inventory. At this point don't bother thinking about the self-inflicted distractions, such as playing music or talking on the phone, while you're playing poker online. Just consider all the input that's coming at you all the time. Think about how different this input is from what you find in a real-world poker environment.

_____

_____

From where I sit, I can see out a window. This in and of itself sets my online poker lair apart from most real-world cardrooms. Mostly when I look out the window, I see the same old stuff: flowers, trees, a street. But now here comes a car along the street. Or no, not a car, a truck. A FedEx delivery truck. I wonder if it's coming to my house. Nope, it's moving on up the street. No FedEx goodies for JV today. Dang. And I was hoping that Amazon.com would deliver my new Counting Crows CD today. Oh, plus there's that check that guy said he was sending. Did he say FedEx or snail mail? I forget. Perhaps I should call him. Or maybe e-mail. Or . . .

Oops, did I get distracted? Sorry.

See how it happens? See how easy? Folks, I'm not playing online poker here, I'm just writing a book; if my mind wanders to visions of FedEx goodies, it has cost me nothing but a little bit of time. But if I were playing online poker and I allowed my mind to wander, I'd certainly miss something, and it might be something crucial.

Continue your inventory. List all the darts of distraction that pierce your concentration even if you kill the stereo and turn off the phone and shut the door and hang out the "Do not disturb on pain of dismemberment" sign.

I hear the overhead fan humming softly, and the fan in my computer humming at a whole different pitch. I see the lights on my printer. I should turn that off; I'm not using it right now. I feel that lump in the seat of my desk chair and remind myself that I've been thinking of getting a new chair. I note a stack of bills to the left of my desk and chide myself for not paying those. I look at the system clock on my computer—it's running slow again. I wonder why that is . . .

You might find my obsessive attention to this sort of detail meaningless and quaint. I might not even argue the point with you, except to say that this sort of detail is present *whether you attend to it or not.* You are aware of the system clock and the computer fan and the overhead fan and the unpaid bills. Maybe not consciously aware, but aware just the same. These things steal your focus in tiny increments, but the increments add up. To take that focus back, simply bring your total awareness of your total environment up to the conscious level. The thief can't strike while you're looking.

In practical terms, you can't purify your environment. You can't purge it of distractions any more than you can purge the b&m environment of its cocktail runners or chip runners or keno runners or bet runners. But in the b&m realm, you can turn your attention to the table, and the table provides enough sensory information to blur the background distractions. Here in your home environment, that will not be the case. Simply put, you can't stare hard enough at the computer screen to make the window go away. The best you can do is to be aware of the window and say, "Don't bother me now, I'm busy."

You may think I'm being flip, but believe me I'm not. Online poker is a serious business, at least if you're doing it right. Many is the player who has entered lightly into a relationship with the online game and suffered financial beats accordingly. So consider my exercises quaint and meaningless if you desire, but *do them just the same*. Become aware of your environment. It's how you hold it at bay. Remember, in this realm, your computer screen is a tiny, tiny fraction of your total data stream. It fights an uphill battle. You want to fight *with* it, not *against* it.

For instance, though you can't perfectly purge your end of the online environment, you can certainly clean up the neighborhood. When you sit down to play poker online, your visual field should be free of anything unrelated to poker. Move the bills and the tax forms and the other paperwork out of sight. Have a comfortable chair to sit in, with your pointing device in comfortable reach. Especially if you're going to be playing online for many, many hours, it's important that you have good physical comfort. Otherwise, fatigue will take its toll.

Clean up the audio environment too. Turn off the radio, stereo, and TV. Many players find this step especially hard to take, believing they can easily play online poker and listen to a ball game, say, with one ear. They may be right, but I hazard to guess that they're trying to solve a problem they don't even know they have: understimulation. Since the poker information coming from the computer screen is so limited, many online players feel as if *there's just not enough going on* when they play online, and they seek to fill that void by adding music or television to the mix. They think they're doing no harm, but I suspect they're wrong. If the background hum of a computer fan can steal your focus, imagine what Nine Inch Nails can do!

Understimulation, in its broadest terms, is a big pitfall for many players. They just don't feel as if there's enough going on on-screen to hold their attention, so they seek more: more input, more data, more noise. If you feel as if you just can't do without the soundtrack, I have to ask what you really want out of your online poker experience. Do you just want to be entertained? If so, then by all means fill your ears with every conceivable sound. Keep filling them until your head explodes. But if your goal is to play a good game of poker and reap the rewards, then you'd better focus on what you're doing. And focus starts where self-indulgence ends.

So here is the online poker environment: at once rich in distraction and poor in stimulation. The advantage of the online poker environment is that you can *control* it. So shut the door . . . pull up a comfortable chair . . . turn off the stereo . . . and focus on the task at hand. That's how winning poker starts in the Internet game.

PLANNING YOUR ONLINE SESSION

Conscientious poker players do a lot of pre-planning before they attack a poker game in a cardroom or casino. I know one Las Vegas pro who sleeps till 3:00 A.M. every weekend morning, then goes out to attack games he knows will be full of tired, drunk, and tilty tourists. Naturally you can't employ this strategy online—it's only 3:00 A.M. in your time zone—but there are other sorts of steps you can take to make sure that your online session is a productive and well-played one.

Before I get to those steps, let's pause a moment and consider the opposite situation: the unplanned session. The willingness to play online without adequate preparation represents a hole in many players' games. Let's see how it happens.

Okay, let's see how it happens with me.

I've been writing all day. Good day, productive day, I churned out a lot of words. Now I'm done with all those words and ready for a little diversion. I think I might like to set my sights on a shorthanded hold'em game. I haven't really thought it through or anything—I just think I might. So I close my word processor and in the time it takes to say "Open poker program," I'm logged on and scanning the available tables for a game. I don't find the game I'm looking for, but I do find exactly the game I'm *not* looking for. It's one with too many strong players at too high a limit for my moderate bankroll. I don't care. I have made the decision—the *commitment*—to play online, and I'm not going to let such a little complication as playing over my head against quality opponents stop me. I didn't come all the way from . . . well, right here . . . to back off now.

Can you see what a mistake this is? Can you see how easily it's made? The brain yields utterly and thoughtlessly to the impulse to play poker. The ease of access to the online game makes executing that decision quick and painless—so quick and so painless that planning and common sense have no chance to catch up. If I'm not careful (and in this realm it's so easy *not* to be careful), I'm in a big psychological hole before I see my first flop—and likely a big financial hole soon after.

Planning is everything. Before you sit down to play, think about the following things:

- What type(s) of game do you want to play?
- What limits are you willing to play?
- Do you prefer tournaments or cash games?
- Do you favor many or few opponents?
- How much will you buy in for?
- How long will you play?

This last question is possibly the most important because one problem with online sessions is figuring out how to end them. It helps if you have a clear idea of how long you intend to contend. *I'm going to play for one hour or 50 hands or until I double through or until the 11:00 news comes on.* Interestingly, if we were contemplating this question in a b&m, we'd probably say something like, *"I'm going to play as long as the game is good."* This strategy doesn't serve us well online because there's *always* a good game somewhere, and getting there is merely a matter of mouse clicks.

Take a moment to describe to yourself the ideal terms and conditions of your online poker session. Do you want the spouse out of the house? The kids in bed asleep? The more thought and detail you put into this ideal model, the easier it will be for you to make the real terms of your play conform to your ideal.

_____

_____

The next step in your planning is the elimination of the aforementioned distractions. Turn off the phone and stereo. Close the other applications on your computer. Make it clear to those around you that you're going to play poker now, and create the expectation that you are not to be frivolously disturbed. This last part may be difficult to sell. *Why can't daddy be disturbed? He's only playing poker?* Well, if you were playing poker in a b&m cardroom, your loved ones would hardly expect you to drop everything at the first casual request. Impress upon them that the money at stake online is every bit as real as the money you'd put into a live game. Moreover, make it clear that this is *not* play and this is *not* a game; it's a serious attempt, seriously constructed, to suck money from the Internet.

Now make it clear to yourself.

Take a moment to remind yourself of what you want out of online poker. If all you want is recreation, and the odd chance to pocket a bean or two, then fine, you don't need to bother preparing and you don't even need to turn off the TV. But if you want to win money, then you need to psych up yourself, set aside your distractions, and settle in for your session with an unyielding single-mindedness of purpose. And hey, guess what? Even if your only goal is to enjoy yourself, you'll probably enjoy yourself more if you're properly prepared. You can take pleasure in a game plan well conceived and executed. No matter how seriously or frivolously you take your online poker, it can hardly be argued that playing badly is more fun than playing well.

So then, planning: give yourself a mental briefing before you start. (Take a walk around the block to clear your head before you start if it helps.) Warn those around you of your intention to concentrate on your game for now. Remind yourself that focus is not a set-and-forget function; it's something you have to attend to hand after hand after hand. Know what game and what stakes you're going for, and know how long you plan to stay.

As to this latter matter, there are two types of sessions

you should try to avoid: those too short, and those too long.

The short session, or *hit-and-run*, is favored by some on-line players, who think that they can jump into a game, push people around with bully behavior, and get out again before the others can adjust or recover. In most cases this is not the strategic execution of a game plan so much as a rationalization for playing "just a few hands" when time does not allow longer play. It's easy to see how this sort of thinking can go wrong. Suppose you jump into a game for a blitzkrieg only to run into a couple of tough or lucky players who put you into a fast, deep hole. You will have turned *hit-and-run* into *hit-and-run bad*, and you'll either leave the game feeling rotten or stick around trying to get well, even though you had no intention (or time) to play a long session in the first place.

Notice that hit-and-run is a phenomenon peculiar to the online environment. While players in the real world may jump around from game to game, it's the rare poker aficionado who will drive any distance (even five miles) to play only five minutes, then turn around and go home. Nor is it considered particularly polite to hit-and-run in the real world. Online, no one cares. So what if you leave after five hands? Your seat will be filled in an instant.

Opposite to the hit and run is the marathon session, and while real-world players are no strangers to all-nighters, the online marathon has its own special qualities. First, it's easy to get hooked. Unlike in the real-world game, where everyone has to go home sometime, you don't have to go home, for you *are* home, and you can stay as long as you like.

Nor does the game ever break. In the real world, you may be stuck and bleeding, and prepared to go all night, but if everyone else goes home, it's *game over* for you. Online, well, even if everyone evacuates www.inconceivable-poker.com, they're still in action over at www.bragrat.com, so you can just jump over and play there. At some point you become a hamster on an exercise wheel; you might *never* get off.

That's why it pays to plan when to quit before you start.

How long should your online session be? Well, how much time, focus, energy, and stamina do you have? Remember that you're seeing a lot more hands online than you would in the real world. This, as it were, density of poker will take its toll on you. If you're looking for a rule of thumb, try this: since you're seeing maybe twice as many hands as you would in a cardroom, plan to play maybe half as long. And don't forget to take breaks along the way. Click that "sit out" button at least once an hour and get up and stretch your legs. After all, you're becoming weary in two ways: your mind is getting fatigued from all that poker, while meanwhile all that sitting in front of a computer is doing your body no favors.

You know, a lot of poker players take pains to remind themselves that it doesn't matter if they win or lose *today*. They treat their poker sessions as parts of one long session, and measure their performance over time. You'll hear such players say, "I don't have to play more now; the game will be there tomorrow." While that's true in the b&ms, it's *really* true on the Internet. Since online poker caught on several years ago, there hasn't been a *single second* when a cash money game wasn't happening *somewhere* in cyberspace. So if you find yourself extending a session because you're afraid you'll never find a game this good again, consider the possibility that, well, you're lying. You're extending the session because *you just don't want to quit*. That's fine, that's up to you. If you want to play all night, play all night. Just don't do it on the pretext that the opportunity will go away if you don't exploit it now. That opportunity isn't going *anywhere.*

The crucial thing is to be the one exploiting the opportunity of others' bad play, not the opportunity being exploited by them.

Take a moment to devise a strategy or two for putting a time cap on your online sessions. Put it in context of your other life activities, and look for a time hole sufficient to meet your playing needs, but at the same time constrained or closed-ended (an hour of play before church on Sunday, e.g.).

BOLD VERSUS CARELESS

It's easy to be bold on the Internet. No one can see you sweat. If you bluff, they can't look in your eyes and register your fear that they'll call. Shaking hands don't give you away; *nothing* gives you away. Many players who have difficulty "selling" an image in the real world appreciate the fact that on the Internet they don't have to. And for many players, poker is a fantasy of boldness to begin with. Never having been bullies in their everyday life, they enjoy the bully behavior of using cards, chips, and betting muscle to push other players around. Cloaked in the anonymity of online play, these would-be bullies enjoy boldness squared. Maybe you enjoy it, too, and maybe it's the strength of your game.

Just don't let boldness veer off into carelessness. You get used to clicking that "raise" button too many times, and clicking that "raise" button becomes not a considered poker decision, but just a habit you have. Also, given the pace of Internet play, it's—literally—hard to slow down. Get into raising wars on the Internet, and you'll find the chips flying farther, faster, and—hand for hand—much longer than in a real-world game. Part of this has to do with the maniac feedback loop discussed before, but much of it has to do with your own state of mind. When the bets and raises are flying, but the only effect you see is a changing number on your screen, it's easy to stop caring where that number goes.

Mike Caro, author of *Caro's Book of Tells*, talks about a player's threshold of pain. He points out that after a player has lost a certain amount, he won't feel very much more pain even if he loses *a lot* more money. This threshold of pain is much lower, and much more easily passed on the Internet than in a real-world game. The pace of play, the "unreality" of Internet bets, and your own fantasy sense of self conspire to make it so. To top it all off, when the losses do start coming, they can come so fast—hand after hand after relentless and unstoppable hand—that the whole thing starts to seem unreal. You can get caught in a negative vortex of the worst possible kind where fast losing breeds rash chasing, which leads to more fast losing and more rash chasing. Before you know it, you're in a hole that you'll need weeks of careful, considered play to climb out of.

Who needs that?

Guard against carelessness in two ways. First, remember that those cyberbets once were dollars in your pocket, and it is hoped that one day they will be again. Respect them— always respect them as the real, spendable bucks they are. Second, *play the game, don't let the game play you*. The online environment can create its own frenzied momentum. If no one else seems to care about his money, it's easy for you to stop caring, too. It's also easy to convince yourself that this is a beatable game. Maybe it is, if you have the time and the patience to do it right. But if the pace of play, coupled with the high volatility of a frenzied table, will cost you more than you can stand to lose, *get out.* Don't worry about looking bad or losing face. You have no face, remember—only a screen name and maybe an avatar. Don't worry about losing income. Another game, even more to your liking, is out there waiting for you right now.

When I teach writing to writers, I encourage them to write meaningful notes to themselves, such as *procrastinate later* or *practice makes progress,* and post these notes where the writers can see them, and be inspired by them, in the course of their writing sessions. We could fruitfully apply the same strategy to our Internet poker sessions, as a means of policing our ongoing state of mind. What would it hurt to post yourself a little note such as *Have you passed the point of pain?* It might save you from one of those all-too-familiar Internet holes that are easy to dig and oh so hard to fill.

MULTITASKING

I took a lot of writing classes in college, classes which only required that I sit and listen. Only I found that I couldn't feel comfortable just sitting and listening. There just wasn't enough *going on* to keep my mind busy. I had a tendency to fall asleep. That's when I learned about embroidery. Once I made my hands busy, the rest of me was content to sit and listen. I had discovered multitasking, and it's a tool that has served me well.

Many online players turn to multitasking as a means of bridging the gaps in online poker. Though the time between hands is incredibly small—a matter of seconds—that time hangs too heavily on some players' hands. So they fill the time between hands, and even the time between bets, with other activities. This is not so different from multi-tasking in the b&ms, where you'll find players reading the newspaper or watching TV or chatting with friends or doing a crossword puzzle while waiting for the next deal. We know that these players are making a mistake: they should be concentrating on the game.

But multitasking isn't always a mistake in the online environment. It can guard against looseness. That is, if you can't stand to be out of action for even a few seconds, you're likely to call with garbage, just so you don't have to *freaking wait!* Unless you have something else to do. In a perfect world, you wouldn't need something else to do. You would be able to play your hand properly, lay it down appropriately, study the other players for the rest of the hand, and rejoin the action on the next deal. But for reasons already mentioned—the way that information comes to you online—it's easy to let your mind wander. While neither path is perfect, it's probably better to let your mind wander than to let your calling requirements vanish. So if you can't have perfect concentration, a distraction will do in a pinch.

One dangerous form of multitasking, a form that only online play affords, is the possibility of playing two games at once. After all, on a big computer screen there's ample room there to display two tables. Why not take another seat somewhere? That way you'll almost always be in action, right? And the sites don't stop you. They don't care how many seats you fill as long as you have money for each. After all, if there are two of you playing in their games, that's two of you paying a rake. You're two customers in one! And even if the sites did ban it, what could stop a player from having two different games going on two different sites? That's right . . . nothing. Nothing, that is, except his own self-interest.

Some players think double-dipping is a great idea. They reckon that playing in two games gives them twice the opportunity to win, and it would if (a) they were winning players to begin with (most aren't), and (b) they could adequately contend in two games at once (most can't). But if concentration is a problem, playing two games at once can seem like a solution. It certainly does focus your concentration; you're following action, posting blinds, looking for tells, and making moves in two games at the same time. That's a *ton* of activity. There's *always* something going on, something that demands your attention.

If you've ever walked in a creek bed, you know that it can be difficult to move slowly and carefully from boulder to boulder. You risk losing your balance and falling in. Alternatively, more effectively, if you build up a little momentum, you can more or less fall forward along the stream bed. Double-dipping creates this same sense of falling forward. While it lasts, the sheer momentum of the thing can make you feel as if you have a great grasp of both games.

The question is, can it last? Are you really so good a player, so much better than your opponents, that you can afford to spread your skills and your attention over two games at once? Are you really so adept at following the action that you can pick up every little nuance in both games? Are you so arrogant as to believe you'll never miss something critical?

Then there's the rudeness factor. If you're stewing over a decision in one game, you may be holding up the action in the other. You do owe a debt of courtesy to the other players. It's not fair to slow them down just because playing one game at a time doesn't hold your focus.

Those who double dip regularly don't care about arrogance, and they sure don't care about rudeness. They do it for a simple, self-serving reason: it's *fun*! No doubt about it, the challenge of handling two games at once can create an exhilarating buzz. But buzz is not why we play poker. No, we play to win money, and while we might rationalize that double-dipping is enhancing our performance, the opposite is more likely true.

Consider . . .

You're a big-limit player, but there are no big-limit games going on right now. So you slum down to the $3–$6 game, looking for action. You know you can't loosen up your standards *too* much, but it's just too boring to sit there and wait for good hands to wash up on your screen, especially when the entire pot at this limit is no more than a bet or two in the games you regularly play.

So you decide to sit down in another game. You figure that at this limit your foes are all monkeyfish anyhow, and you can beat them—literally—with one lobe tied behind your brain. But now comes a moment when you get playable hands in both games. Do you remember which table features the Cally Wallies and which table holds the bluff-raisers? Should you check? Raise? Fold? Which? *Where?* You only have a few seconds to decide, and both games want you to decide *right now*! And it happens again and again.

Next thing you know, you've dropped a hundred in one game and a hundred in the other, and that's not play money; that's work money—money you're going to have to *work* to win back elsewhere. How do you like your strategy now?

I and almost every online player I know have tried double-dipping at least once. We've discovered—and you'll discover, because you'll inevitably try it too—that it is exciting and stimulating but not conducive to great play. If concentration is your problem, you won't solve that problem by soaking it in adrenaline. Double-dipping is simply not the answer.

Is there an answer? Should you keep a crossword puzzle on your desk or file your nails between hands? While I don't recommend self-distraction of any kind, if multitasking is necessary to keep your play in line, then multitasking it is. Just make sure you choose an activity that won't make you miss crucial game information as you go.

Embroidery, for example. I have some lovely patterns you might try.

6

DATA MANAGEMENT

♣ ♠ ◇ ♡

Many people dismiss out of hand the idea of Internet poker because they can't see their foes' faces, and thus feel that they'll never have a decent read. They believe that without human interaction, something irreplaceable is lost, something so intrinsic that its lack renders the whole exercise pointless. What these people overlook is the vast amount of information available to the online player that's just completely and totally not available in the b&m game. This chapter looks at these abundant data streams and examines ways to exploit them to our advantage. I think you'll find that what you gain in data at least balances out what you lose in direct visual tells.

COMMIT TO HANDICAPPING YOUR FOES

Suppose you're holding Big Maxx (K♣ Q♣) and your online opponent bets into a board of K-6-3. You think you have the best hand, but you're not sure. Would this foe, you wonder, bet only A-K in this situation, or would he take a flier on K-J or K-T? Is he sufficiently weak to have gotten in-

volved with K-6 or K-3? In the real world, you'd call for
time, stare into his eyes, and try to get some kind of read
on him. You might even succeed. This option is obviously
not available to you online—you can't see the player's eyes.
But what you *can* see is this little notebook here on your
desk, a notebook containing everything you've ever ob-
served about this foe. And hey, lo and behold, he has demonstrated a strong willingness in the past to push big cards
with medium kickers. Based on the information at hand,
you conclude that that's what he's doing now. So you
reraise. He calls, then calls you down the rest of the way,
only to find his K-J losing to your K-Q. You chalk up the
victory—and record what you've just learned in your notebook for next time.

What online poker offers is just an insane amount of
cold, hard data about your foes—data that you can accumulate, sort, store and, best of all, refer to *while you play*.
Just imagine trying to do this in a b&m game.

*Hmm . . . You just reraised a button raise from the big blind.
Are you aggressively defending your blind, or do you have a
real hand? Time, please, while I flip through my notebook
and see what you've done in the past.*

In the words of the sage, "That dog don't hunt." Yet this
is exactly the sort of reference work you can do in an online game. And it's exactly the sort of reference work your
best opponents are doing on you.

If you're serious about online poker, you'd better get serious about the idea of handicapping your foes, exactly as a
serious horseplayer seriously handicaps horses. And just as
a good horseplayer makes money on the margin between
his interpretation of data and the next guy's, you will make

money in direct proportion to your willingness and ability to keep book on your foes.

Herein lies the single biggest difference between online poker and real-world poker: in the real-world game, poker skill is what separates money winners from money losers over time. In the online game, it's a combination of poker skill and *data management*. What you do with your data is huge, just huge.

Say you're playing against some players whom you have matched wits with many times before. In a real-world game, you'd have a "feel" for these guys, a sense of who plays a good, solid game, and who gets frisky or out of line. In the online game, thanks to the notes you've taken, you have much more solid information to go on than just a "feel." Your records indicate, for instance, that billybob from Toledo has only raised twice in the hundreds of hands he's played against you, and both times he had pocket aces. He raises now. What hand do you put him on? Yep, pocket aces. You muck your pocket jacks and save yourself a butt-load of bets.

Now here comes Flippy from Finland betting into a scary flop of A-A-K. Consulting your records, you find that Flippy has made this sort of play many times before. He likes to exercise the right of first bluff to try to steal this kind of pot, but your records indicate that he's folded many times in the face of a reraise here. So you pop him back and Flippy packs it in.

Information, as they say, is power. In some circumstances it's the power of *knowing absolutely* how your opponents will behave.

Information, alas, is work as well. That is, it will take a certain amount of effort to collect, collate, and interpret the information that online poker offers you. Maybe you don't feel like doing this work. Maybe it just seems like more trouble than it's worth. After all, if your information only gives you the advantage of one or two bets over the course of a session, how much benefit is that, really? Not much—if you're just hacking around. But if you want to *win,* and more particularly if you want to be a *skillful, capable player,* then this is the sort of work you'll do. And even if it only pays the money dividend of a couple of bets a session (no negligible sum over time, of course) it also pays you dividends in terms of skill and self-respect. Having invested time and effort in using online data to your advantage, you get to see yourself as someone capable of doing this kind of work and making it pay. This benefits not just your bankroll but your outlook and your life as a whole. Further, if attention deficit disorder is your online poker problem, devoting yourself to data will make that problem go completely and totally away. Put simply, there's *always* information to glean from the screen. There's *always* something to keep your eager mind busy. All you have to do is commit to keeping track.

If the mental wherewithal to make this commitment still eludes you, think once more about that skilled horse handicapper. Because of pari-mutuel betting, he knows that his success depends on the failure of other bettors. He knows, and expects, that some will bet the favorite because it's the favorite, and that others will bet number three because three is their lucky number, and that still others will bet HereComesTheBride because they were married once, or at least their wives were. The savvy handicapper knows that his profits come directly from the "dead money" that these imperfect decision makers put into the pari-mutuel pool. Likewise, a skilled poker player knows that most of his profit comes from the poor decision-making skills of his opponents. But the *online* poker player can actually increase this margin simply by backing up his decisions with excellent data. He knows that most of his foes will be too lazy to bother doing this, and he knows that if he just works as hard as the most diligent horse handicappers, he'll make money on the margin.

So you have to ask yourself (to quote Dean Reisner who wrote these words for Clint Eastwood), "Do I feel lucky? Well, do ya, punk?" You'd better feel lucky, because luck is the only thing that will save you when others come after you armed with intimate information about the way you have played in the past.

GAME SELECTION

Okay, you've decided to make data management part of your online skill-set. A good place to start is in the area of table selection. You already know that choosing the right table is crucial to success in poker; thanks to the information provided by the site, it's easy for the online player to make great decisions in this area. Just look at all the data the sites give for free:

- The number of players at the table and the number of players waiting
- Average number of players seeing each flop
- Average pot size
- The number of hands dealt per hour

Note that not all sites provide all this information, and consider this difference when deciding where to put your real money into play. After all, if you're going to be the sort of player who uses information as power, it only makes sense to play on those sites that amplify your edge by giving you the most information to use.

Now, let's say that you want to play $5–$10 hold'em, and you're looking at the following sign-up board:

TABLE	STAKES	AVERAGE PLAYERS PER FLOP	AVERAGE DOLLARS PER POT	HANDS PER HOUR	NUMBER OF PLAYERS
Grumpy	$5–$10	58 percent	$45	69	9
Happy	$5–$10	33 percent	$37	73	9
Sleepy	$5–$10	23 percent	$42	92	9
Dopey	$5–$10	23 percent	$26	82	9
Doc	$5–$10	40 percent	$50	58	9

Based on just this information, which would you take to be the best game? That's right: table Grumpy, for the simple reason that more players are seeing the flop. It's not the richest game at this moment, but it looks like the loosest, so that's where you'd want to go . . . unless there's a much better opportunity waiting for you at a different limit or over on the Omaha/8 board. Have you looked? Be sure to examine all relevant options before jumping into the first available seat. There's almost always a terrifically rich and loose game out there waiting for you somewhere.

And once you have a seat in a game, don't forget to go back and check the board periodically for new opportunities. The composition of online games changes so quickly that what may have seemed like a dull, plodding game a little while ago has morphed into a gold mine now. Thanks to the mechanics of online play, it's a snap to switch games in pursuit of the greenest possible pastures.

A word of caution: though this information is important, don't put *too much* stock in it. For instance, if all five tables are showing see-the-flop percentages in the 20 percent to 30 percent range then they're all about equally tight, and you don't have to choose the one with the absolutely highest number of pre-flop callers. Also remember that the composition of the table will change. It may become tighter or looser, and that change can happen very quickly. Just as you're constantly monitoring the sign-up board for a better game, keep monitoring the game you're in to make sure that it's still as good as you want it to be.

Nor should you necessarily take the stats at face value or make assumptions about how they're derived. Consider average number of players per flop. On some sites, that average is computed over the life of the table, from the first hand forward. On other sites, it's only the average for the last ten hands. In the former case, a high number indicates that the table has historically been loose. In the latter case, it means that the table is loose *right now*. To find out how those averages are computed, you'll have to send e-mails to technical support and ask. Don't be afraid to do so. Remember what the squeaky wheel gets.

Over time, you will discover that the composition of the table—the individual players you find there—is more important than players per flop or hands per hour. Once you have data on a good number of a site's regular players, you'll be able to refine your choice of table based on who's there—and who isn't. The presence of a proven Cally Wally, for example, can make the difference in choosing between two statistically similar games. Likewise, there may be fish galore at a certain table, but if the table already contains a couple of sharks (known to you as such because you've got book on them) you may be better off elsewhere.

As an exercise, spend some time scouting the sign-up board and practice handicapping the games. If you have a friend or fellow player, handicap the same games and see whether your assessments line up. Identify what you consider to be the best and the worst tables—then remind yourself that there's no need, ever, to play in an unpromising game.

A number of online players don't give a fig about the average pot size or the number of players seeing the flop. All they care about is the number of players at the table. They go looking for shorthanded games because they know (or believe) themselves to be excellent shorthanded players. If that's you, that's fine—go after those shorthanded games, using the sign-in board to help you find them. Just don't forget to go back and look for new alternatives if the game you've elected to join starts to get full. A juicy shorthanded game can become unprofitably crowded in a scant matter of minutes.

HAVING BOOK

Having book in the context of online poker (not to be confused with *making book* in the context of the Michigan-Michigan State football game) is the act of assembling, sorting, and using information about the way our online opponents play. Having book, then, is online poker slang for *doing our homework*, but if we called it *doing our homework*, we likely wouldn't do it at all, so we call it *having book* instead.

When you have book on your foes, you have a detailed record of many things: how much money they usually buy in for, how much they bought in for this time, how long they generally play, how long they've been playing today, what they'll do with their blinds, whether they're capable of check-raising or check-raise bluffing, and a host of other powerful predictors of future behavior.

Many intuitively adroit players have good intuitive book on their foes, and knowing what their foes are likely to do in certain situations is what makes these players the winners they are. The good news about online poker is that in this realm you don't have to be intuitively adroit. You don't need to be able to remember an opponent's tendencies or calling requirements. You don't need to remember *anything*. You can write it all down and keep it on your desk when you play online. A good book on your foes reduces online poker to the equivalent of an open-book exam; you don't have to have the answers in your head, 'cause you can always look 'em up.

Having book also keeps your head in the game. Even though you've folded your hand, you still have something to do, for every deal offers data on *someone*. The hunt for this data will keep your attention where it belongs, fixed squarely on the screen. It may even solve that pesky problem of understimulation. Though you're having to fold hand after hand after hand, you might not be bored if your hunt for information yields the treasure of a player's tendency to go too far with bottom pairs or slim draws.

You will develop your most valuable book on players you face regularly because they will reveal themselves to be in general either foes you can beat or those who can beat you, and this information will help you pick the right game from among available options. It will also help your decision making within a session. Consider this situation: You're in the big blind when player pasquale52 raises, and you're wondering whether to defend. Your records indicate that once pasquale52 starts betting, he rarely lets up. You might decide to let this blind go, rather than tangle with such an aggressive bettor. But on your next blind, the raise comes from EmilioEarhart, and your book tells you that this player will only bet a flop that hits his hand. Here you have a much more productive call because you can take the pot with a bet on a subsequent street if EmilioEarhart misses his hand.

Your book is your best friend. It tells you whom to mess with and whom to leave alone. It keeps your brain riveted to the task at hand. It deepens your understanding of poker and poker situations. It makes you smarter. (The mere act of writing stuff down makes you smarter.) Book is especially good news for players who don't have terrific memory for players or their plays. Can't recall whether Li'l Abner from Dogpatch likes to bluff at uncontested pots? Good news! You don't have to remember. Your book remembers for you.

It's worth keeping book on opponents you're facing for the first time and may never face again, and not just because it keeps your head in the game. Even within a single session it's useful to know, for example, whether a player is running well or not. If you have book on him, you know how much he had at the table when you or he entered the game, and you can compare that figure with how he's doing now. If joefromchicago was sitting on $200 when you entered the game, and he's down to $50 now, you can be pretty sure that he's either unskilled or unlucky. In either case, the fact that he's running bad right now makes him a prime target.

Dependence on book can be a tiny problem. You might become so reliant on having pertinent information at your fingertips that you no longer bother storing such data in your brain. Then, when you go into the b&ms, where having and keeping book is impractical, and possibly not even allowed, your lack of onboard information might work to your disadvantage. This is another divergence between the online game and the real-world game. The real-world game places a huge premium on your detailed memory of your opponents' past performances. For an online player, a well-maintained book completely neutralizes this edge.

If you're inclined to trust just your memory anyway, I would point out that keeping book is, in a sense, just keeping up with the Joneses. Your most dedicated foes are busy keeping book on you. If you're not busy keeping book on them, you'll find yourself at a huge disadvantage, a disadvantage you're not likely to overcome by means of luck or looks or even skill. What good is your skill if your best opponents can anticipate all your best moves?

Got book? If you plan to be a winning player, the answer had better be yes.

BASIC BOOK

The most basic book is a brief record of when each player enters the game and how much money he brings. To chart this information, just get a small notebook with lots of pages and assign the left-hand side of two facing pages to each player (the reason for which follows). When you first join a game, create an entry for every player already at the table, then just add pages as new players come in. A sample page in your notebook might start out looking like this:

> BlackAdder from London
>
> 3/25/03, 10:50 p.m.
> $3–$6 hold'em, $150

You won't collect all the same information for every player. In the example just given, we know that BlackAdder is (or claims to be) from London. This information might be useful if we find ourselves playing against BlackAdder when it's 9:00 P.M. in Los Angeles, and therefore the middle of the night where he is. What's he doing up at that hour? Is he stuck and tilty? Insomniac? Just waking up? We can't know, of course, just as we can't know he's telling the truth about being from London, so maybe this information doesn't help us. If he claims to be from Mars or the back of your closet, though, you know that the information is irrelevant and you won't bother recording it.

Wherever he's from, you now have a baseline on his play. You know how long you and he have shared a table, and you know how your relative stacks started out. It's not always possible to note how much money a player cashed out with, for the simple reason that he may be gone without warning. But if you can see, and note, a player experiencing a big shift in money, that tells you whether he's a winner today. Book his sessions over time, and you can deduce whether he's a regular contributor or winner. Soon, as your book grows, you'll know who the regulars are at your site and your betting limit.

Here's my book on BlackAdder after five encounters:

<u>BlackAdder</u> from London

3/25/03, 10:50 p.m.
$3–$6 hold'em, $150

3/26/03, 9:15 a.m.
$3–$6 hold'em, $90
   quit at 9:30, down $60

3/28/03, 10:15 a.m.
$5–$10 hold'em, $50(!)
   he joined the game with this amount

4/1/03

$5–$10 hold'em, $349

4/10/03

$2–$4 hold'em, $35

Taken in sum, this snapshot of BlackAdder identifies him to me as a low-limit player who hasn't shown any particular aptitude for winning and has, on at least one occasion, made the identifiable mistake of buying in to a higher limit game for not nearly enough money. Note that I will amplify my raw data as necessary, in this case recording the fact of his terrible short buy into the $5–$10 game.

Now then, I've created an entry on the left-hand side of two facing pages. What do I plan to do with the right-hand side? Well, there I'm going to record anecdotal evidence about the player's performance. I might jot down hands he reveals (noting position or circumstances if I can). I will rate his aggressiveness, using a scale of 1 to 5, 1 being least aggressive and 5 being most. I can change this number, of course, if he changes his behavior, but in my experience online players don't really vary their aggressiveness that much: they either generally are or generally aren't predisposed to bully behavior.

I want to know whether a player will fold his blind in the face of a raise, so I chart his behavior in that area. I want to know if he's capable of bluffing or check-raising, so I record that. Anything I note about his play (such as a tendency to raise with drawing hands) I'll write down. No single piece of information may be useful, but taken as a whole, a pretty firm picture of the player quickly starts to emerge.

BlackAdder from London

3/25/03, 10:50 p.m.
$3–$6 hold'em, $150

3/26/03, 9:15 a.m.
$3–$6 hold'em, $90
    quit at 9:30, down $60

3/28/03, 10:15 a.m.
$5–$10 hold'em, $50 (!)
    he joined the game with
    this amount

4/1/03
$5–$10 hold'em, $349

4/10/03
$2–$4 hold'em, $35

BlackAdder from London

Hands I've seen: A-K, K-Q, 3-4s
(suited), 4-8 (late position, unraised multi-way pot, 8-8 (raise)

Aggressiveness: 4

Blind fold: yes

Bluff: ✓✓✓✓

Check-raise: ✓✓

Raises with straight & flush
draws—Raise/fold—Likes real
estate raises—Will change seats
to gain position—Exposes bluffs
for advertising—Active chatter

I have now identified BlackAdder as a fairly aggressive player who bluffs a lot and is capable of releasing his blind. I've seen him push his draws and I've seen him fold in the face of a reraise. I know him to be someone who will make real estate raises—bets of opportunity in late position. As time goes by, I will collect more anecdotal evidence and create an ever fuller and more detailed profile of this foe.

Can the information be trusted? Not completely. Can I be confident that BlackAdder will fold every time I raise his blind? No, of course not . . . no more than I could be confident of similar reads on real-world opponents. After all, I only know what he's done in certain situations in the past. I don't know what he'll do in this situation now. But I can guess . . . and my guess is now an educated, not a blind, one.

In any case, compare my picture of BlackAdder with my right-hand page on *Chip Weevil:*

<u>Chip Weevil</u> from Oxnard

Hands I've seen: 8-7, J-3, 3-3, 4-5s, 2-7(!), A-A, K-K

Aggressiveness: 1

Blind fold: ✓✓✓✓ ✓✓✓✓

Bluff: never

Check-raise: never

Checks the nuts—Raises only w/ A-A, K-K—Chases four-outers—Whiney chatter

Now here's a player who's weak, passive, and loose. All the evidence suggests that I'm going to get straightforward play from this guy and never have to worry about nasty surprises like check-raises or check-raise bluffs, because these are plays he has shown no ability to make. If he did throw a check-raise at me sometime, a quick scan of my notebook would tell me to respect that raise and get the hell out of his way unless I had something to go to war with. Again, I can't treat this information as absolutely accurate, but I sure can use it to identify a trend and to recognize when a fellow is going against his type.

In any event, the bottom line is clear: Given the choice of tangling with (a) BlackAdder or (b) Chip Weevil, who would you rather face? Thanks to your book, you *have* a choice. You can target weak foes and avoid strong ones, with confidence that if your read is off, it's off only by degrees.

Should I happen to see a lot of BlackAdder or Chip

Weevil, so much so that they completely fill their two facing pages, then I'll start to log their play in another notebook, one reserved for frequent foes. In this way I can identify who the regulars are. It's interesting to see how players' participation in a site ebbs and flows over time. You might encounter someone only occasionally, and then suddenly he's there so often that he spills over into your frequent foes book—only to vanish from the scene and never be seen again. In this case, as in all cases, the benefit of your written record is clear: you don't have to wonder whether you ever really saw him that often, because you'll have the evidence at hand.

I want to stress that my way of booking my foes is just that: *my* way. I record information that I find pertinent and also in tune with the type of game I play. I record that information in a way that's meaningful to me. You may use my model if it suits you, but I encourage you to develop your own tools, suited to your own means and needs, in developing book on your opponents. Among other benefits, you'll learn what factors you consider important. You'll also deepen and broaden your understanding of both yourself and your foes because you will be *noticing so much more.*

If it suits you to use my notebook approach, by all means do so, but by all means also experiment. Some note takers have success with word processing programs or spreadsheets. One industrious player I know uses two computers, one for her play and one for her notes. Certain online poker sites, such as Paradise, have a built-in note function. Simply click on your opponent's icon, and a little text box opens in which you can record and save your observations.

You can see, then, all sorts of options are available to you, and your first strategy is not likely to be your very best. So sample a few, and remain flexible and open minded before you settle on a system.

One pitfall: When you first start keeping book, you can become so infatuated by it, or swept up in it, that you try to record every little thing. The frantic desire to *miss nothing* can cause you to miss the most important thing: what's going on in the game. Over time you'll become both faster and more discerning. You'll develop shorthands, your own personal code for describing players' activities, and you'll also develop a sense of what really matters and what you can let go by. Do yourself a favor and practice booking your foes at the free-play tables. That way, when you get into a cash game, this skill will already be honed.

ADVANCED BOOK

A joke about Californians goes like this: *Scratch the surface of a Californian and what do you get? More surface.* Not so with book on your foes. The deeper you go into their play, the more you discover about them—and the more you discover *to* discover. Collecting and managing data on online opponents is an endless, and endlessly fascinating, voyage of exploration.

You can, of course, reach a point of diminishing returns with this stuff. While it's possible to glean, for example, that a certain player has raised in early-to-mid position with low pocket pairs 35 percent of the times you've been able to verify his holding, that information is neither completely reliable (because you haven't always been able to verify his holding) nor particularly useful day in and day out, hand after hand after hand.

On the other hand, never forget that this type of analysis pays other dividends. Though a particular piece of information may not be directly useful, it does directly contribute to your overall understanding of particular foes, and of foes in general. It also improves your analytical skill, and makes you a generally sharper, keener, and more thoughtful player. Plus it keeps you away from Tetris between hands. So if you've gotten good at scratching the surface of your opponents, consider using other analytical tools to go even deeper.

Remember that you have hand logs available to you, those line-by-line histories of hands you've played. If you really want to be a wonk about things, you might consider downloading a couple dozen (or a couple hundred) hand logs and studying certain players' play over time. Suppose you've taken a keen interest in seven-card stud player FuzzyLogic, because he seems to be supremely aggressive, but also wildly clueless. After a long joust against him, you download the hand logs for the session and start examining them. Soon, a pattern emerges. Fuzzy *does* seem to be aggressive, but only when he has scare cards on board and no one else is showing particular strength. He's been caught bluffing a few times, and those few times reinforce the pattern: Fuzzy likes to claim unwanted pots. Sometimes he takes them at gunpoint. So, yes, he is aggressive, but no, he's not clueless. Now you know.

Maybe you have a hunch that Omaha/8 player Juwana-Banana is slaphappy for A-2. You *think,* but you're not sure, that she'll call any flop containing even just one low card, in hopes that her runner-runner low will get there. So you study the hand logs, not unlike poring over the Dead Sea Scrolls, and discover that it's true: JuwanaBanana will chase any possible lock low, no matter how slim her draw. What's more, when the low hasn't gotten there, JuwanaBanana has folded a whopping 97 percent of the time. How confident will you now be bluff-betting into a high-only board on the river?

Confidence is what it's all about in poker, and your examination of hand logs or other statistical records can instill within you the confidence that even if your move doesn't work out this time, over time it will. Your book is your secret weapon. It allows you to make plays with impunity, knowing that the stats are on your side. Maybe this time JuwanaBanana will call you down—perhaps she backed into a viable high hand—but in the long run *she will lay it down*. She's giving you a free ride.

But, TANSTAAFL, right? No such thing as a free lunch, or even a free ride. This particular free ride will cost you the hours and hours of work you'll have to do to generate meaningful results. That's time you could spend actually playing poker, right? Who wants to waste that kind of time?

Winners, that's who. People who are passionately committed to beating the online game not through luck or good looks but through use of the statistical evidence that's available to everyone. Certain of your foes fall into this category. Most don't. Most online players are pure recreationalists. They won't bother keeping book on anyone in any sense, because it interferes with their so-called fun. Maybe you fit in that category, too, in which case I say *mazel tov* and God bless. But have you considered that it might just be *even more fun* to crack your foe open like an egg and crawl inside his brain? This is the opportunity that's available to you.

If I have a foe I'm interested in tracking, I build a database just for him, a record of the hands he's played, what he's done, and how those hands have turned out. To facilitate this effort, to keep pace with the play of the game, I have had to develop my own quirky code, an example of which you see here. Translations to follow.

Brooce from Asbury Park

1103025: sb: r, b, c/r, b, AQs

1103026: b: r, wu

1103033: lp: r, b, b, b, 8-8

1103034: mp: r, rr, ch/f

1103038–1103044: so

1103046: bb: ch, ch/c, ch/r, b, AA

1103050: mp: r, b, wu

1103051: ep: r, b, wu

1103052: ep: r, b/f

1103026 is the hand number. I keep track of hand numbers because it gives me a sense of each player's see-the-flop frequency. Over time, this will tell me whether an individual is tight or loose.

SB, BB, EP, MP, LP and *B* refer to the player's position in the hand: small blind, big blind, early position, middle position, late position, and button, respectively. I look for a correlation between position and action. Pure real estate raisers, for example, reveal themselves by consistent late position or button raises but little or no activity from other positions.

C, B, R, RR, Ch, Ch/F, Ch/C and *Ch/R* are actions: call, bet, raise, reraise, check, check/fold, check/call, and check/raise. The commas between each letter identify the streets, so that a sequence like C, B, B, B indicates a flat-call preflop and lead betting on the flop, turn, and river. I'm particularly keen to see whether a player will raise on an early street and check/fold later. This indicates to me a player who gets out ahead of his hand and is then afraid to follow through.

SO means *sat out*. If I see a player sitting out at regular intervals, I know I'm up against an opponent knowledgeable enough to schedule standard breaks.

WU means *won uncontested*. Players who are getting a lot of uncontested wins often turn out to be both fearless and feared. Their aggressiveness is giving them steal opportunities that hit-to-win players do not receive.

At the end of each entry I note the player's holding, if this information is available. (Obviously if he's not involved in the showdown or wins uncontested I'm unlikely to find this out.) The correlation between betting pattern and hand held can be very revealing. Consider this line: *1103046: bb: ch, ch/c, ch/r, b, AA.* Here we had Brooce just checking his pocket aces in the big blind and check-calling the flop to set up a check-raise on the turn and a lead bet on the river. Not exactly the trickiest play in the world, it's at least an attempt at deception. It's the sort of deception you see very often online, especially in low-limit games, where the object is to get the fish on the hook and keep him there through the river. Next time I see this play from Brooce, I'll have a fairly sound reason to smell a rat.

If you're truly obsessive about winning, there will be times when you don't even bother to play. You just sit in on a game populated by foes you're interested in tracking. Pen in hand, or spreadsheet open, you record their bets, folds, calls, and raises. You correlate their betting actions with the hands they show down. As a watcher, you're not distracted by the need to make decisions of your own. As a book-builder, you're no casual railbird just watching the game to pass the time. You're actually a collector: a collector of weapons that your enemies hand you to use against them.

And there are so *many* weapons to collect. A cursory review of hand logs or your own records will reveal, for instance, whether a certain player *ever* lays down a blind. Some *never do.* If you can find one of these relentless defenders, that's free money. Just set up shop behind their blind and raise to isolate with every better-than-average hand. You'll make money on the difference between your quality holdings and their random hands, and make more money by outplaying them on subsequent streets if they turn out to be unskilled in other areas—which indiscriminate blind-defenders generally are.

As an exercise in data management, hunt through some hand logs or track a group of players until you find one who never ever sees fit to surrender a blind. Naturally you'd prefer to attack this player in a shorthanded or heads-up situation, and that situation may not always be available. But if your advanced book has revealed to you a large number of players in this category, you don't have to settle for unfavorable circumstances; you can go shopping for the right player at the right table—and go right after him!

Can you think of a similar specific piece of information which, if determined to be reliable, would be a reliable money-maker over time?

_____

_____

Hatteras Jack plays bad drawing hands out of position. I often see him in there with 7-8 or K-x suited, limping in and hoping to see cheap flops. If he hits a draw, he'll try for a foreclosure raise, check-raising the flop in hopes of a free card on the turn if he needs it. When I deny him that free card, he'll call anyway, then fold on the river if his draw doesn't get there. I don't need cards to beat him; I just need to let him hang himself on his own betting pattern.

It's useful to know whether certain players are consistent winners or losers over time. Nor need you limit this investigation to merely the players you face. When you log on to a site, you can easily generate a list of all the players at your chosen limit or limits and note how much money they have at that point. At the end of your session, go back through the games and see how the players (those still on site) have been doing. Have they won or lost? How much? This information by itself is not statistically valid—no short-term results ever are—but it will become useful over time. If you identify consistent winners and consistent losers, you can avoid the former and confront the latter. You need never put yourself at a disadvantageous table again!

All because you bothered to take a few notes.

Or no, not a few notes. Many, many notes. So many notes that you may find yourself drowning in a sea of unfiltered information. If this happens to you, you can productively cut back, and focus your attention on just a few types of players. The truth is that most online players don't bear watching, either because they play too infrequently to be worth tracking or because their game is so nondescriptly normal that there's nothing extraordinary about them to learn. Here are the three classes of players I track regularly:

• **Regulars.** It's most important to know what to do with the players you encounter most often. Should you engage them or run away? You want to have clear evidence, not hazy, vague recollections, of past performance, so that you can make a confident and well-informed choice.

• **Dangerous Players.** If someone runs over you, even

once, it's best to mark him or her down in your book as a must to avoid. Maybe he got lucky or maybe he really had your number. (Maybe he had a devastatingly good book on you.) It doesn't matter. There are so many bona fide weakies out there that it makes no sense to go to war against someone who has demonstrated the ability to put you on the ropes and keep you there.

• ***Targets of Opportunity.*** Having identified someone as a genuinely dreadful player, you certainly want to be able to find her again. Catch someone making even one serious mistake and you know you're in the company of someone capable of making more such mistakes in the future. You definitely want to be in the neighborhood when that happens. And you can *guarantee* being in the neighborhood on certain sites, because they conveniently list every player on the site at the time. Use this list; it's like excellent sonar for fish.

As for the rest of the players—occasional visitors and the big fat middle of the skill-set—you can pretty much forget about them. Track their activities so that you have the measure of them, and also to advance your own book-making skills, but don't let their presence or absence in a game tip the scales too much one way or another. There are so many fair-to-poor players out there in the ether that they're pretty much interchangeable.

To make sure that your statistics continue to serve you well, be sure to go back and visit your online host's home page from time to time. You might find that they've added some statistical tool or provided new data on their player base. Heck, you might even discover a juicy bonus you'd overlooked. The fact is that once we've downloaded the game software from a site, most of us never visit that site again. This is a mistake. There's frequently new information to be had there, new edge to accumulate. Don't overlook that edge!

We've all been in real-world poker games where a player or two (we try to be one of them) seem to stand head and shoulders above the competition. They're the best, and everybody knows it. Thanks to the hidden strength of your secret weapon, you can stand head and shoulders above your online competition *and they'll never know it!* Picture yourself going into battle armed with data and hard evidence against foes who have nothing going for them but information from the hand they're in or data collected since this session began. You will certainly dominate and crush such foes, for information is power, and the power is all yours.

BOOK YOURSELF

One player at the table whose play you must absolutely monitor and track is you. In any poker game, if you don't have a firm grasp on what you're doing and why you're doing it, you run the risk of big trouble. In b&m games you can only have this grasp in a general sense: you may feel that you're playing with appropriate selective aggression, say, pushing when you should push and running when you should run. Alternatively, you may have the sense of "running bad," or even be aware that you're on tilt. But all of this information comes to you from within, and it comes to you more in an intuitive sense than with any hard-fact reality.

When you play online, however, you can keep book on yourself just as you would on any other player. You can keep absolute track of which hands you play in which positions, how many times you bluff, what percentage of those bluffs are successful, and on and on and *on*. Truly, your book on yourself is a bottomless well of detail. You will never get to the end of what there is to know about you.

Do *you* over-defend your blind? Why not keep track? Find out *exactly* how many times in the course of a session you let your blind go in the face of a raise. Find out *exactly* which hands you consider worthy of defense, or which players you consider worthy of counter-attack.

(It occurs to me that I've raised the issue of over-defending the blinds several times, which may bring two questions to your mind. First, why am I making such a big deal about it? Second, if appropriately protecting one's blinds is that important, what is an appropriate defense? In answer to the first question, I'm making a big deal about it because it happens *so damn often* online. Far more than in a b&m game, probably for the twin reasons of underestimating foes and undervaluing money, the online blind gets defended and defended and *defended*—and with any old cheese at all. As to the second question, I would call your attention to the "around town" strategy outlined in *Killer Poker: Strategy and Tactics for Winning Poker Play.*)

Do you enter a pot with all guns blazing, only to back down to passivity when the flop doesn't come your way? Correlate the number of times you raise pre-flop with the number of times you check/fold on subsequent streets. If you're like many players, that's a significant leak in your play, one that others can easily exploit once they realize you can be pushed off a hand and made to back down. Now *you* will realize it too.

Do you hold on to A-2 in Omaha/8 like Kate clung to Leo in *Titanic*? Are you one of those cockeyed optimists who will stick around for runner-runner draws to half the pot? Wouldn't you like to know if you are? Now you can have the evidence right before your eyes.

In this sense, online poker offers another tremendous advantage over real-world play. It allows us to study *our own* play in a direct, detailed, and intimate way that we'd never get away with at a real-world table. Oh, sure, you can keep a notebook by your side at the b&m; perhaps you've even done so. But with other players looking on, you tend to make your notes brief and cryptic, their utility killed by the natural self-consciousness you feel while you're writing stuff down. That self-consciousness doesn't exist when you're working online. No one can see the notes you take— not on them, and not on you.

So, then, what kind of notes should you take—*must* you take—in order to feel like you're making the most of this golden opportunity?

First and foremost, *track your results*. Keep the same records that you would keep in any b&m game: the number of hours you played, the limit you played at, and your net amount won or lost. Basic record-keeping software such as *Stat King* or *Card Player Analyst* will help you in this area. But heck, a plain old notebook or spreadsheet will tell you whether you're booking wins or not. Remember that there are two kinds of poker players in this world: those who keep honest records of their results, and losers.

Beyond mere wins and losses, you might want to keep track of what sort of hands you play in which position, how you go about playing those hands, and what sort of results you get. After all, having a winning session is one thing, but how you went about booking that win, and how you might refine your strategies in the future, is something altogether else.

There is an absolute requirement for honesty here. If you're not prepared to record your losses faithfully, you'll delude yourself into thinking you're a winning player when you're not. If you're not willing to accept the fact that you play garbage hands, you'll never figure out how to plug that leak, for the simple reason that you can't fix what you deny being broken. For more on the subject of policing your play with honest, detailed, and faithful record keeping see . . . well . . . that book I just mentioned.

Some sites make it ridiculously easy to tell the truth about yourself to yourself, by putting the cold, hard facts of your play at your fingertips. As of this writing, Paradise Poker provides the most comprehensive array of player stats, but I have no doubt that others will follow suit, since this information is such a powerful tool, and therefore lure, to conscientious and dedicated players. At the click of an appropriate button, you can learn:

- The percentage of flops you've seen.
- The percentage of times your action is fold, check, call, bet, raise, or reraise.
- The percentage of hands won and showdowns won.
- The percentage of wins per flop seen.
- The percentage of times you fold on the flop, turn, river, or not at all.

You can download this information directly to your computer and keep a running tab on your play. Over time you will learn as much about yourself as you know about your foes, and given that each player's greatest threat to himself is usually himself, this information will come in damn handy.

And if that's not enough for you, you can take this business of stat mining to the absolute limit by getting your hands on a little piece of software called PokerStat. This software integrates with Paradise Poker and allows the user to download hand histories directly to a program that will sift, sort, collate, correlate, cross-reference, juggle, yodel, and sing. Really quite amazing stuff, and my only gripe is that (as of the familiar *this writing*) it only supports play at Paradise. But again, I'm confident that by the time you read these words, the statistical software available to the online player will be abundant, comprehensive, and truly mind-boggling. You'll be able to analyze your play down to the most microscopic level, and learn the truth of your own poker experience.

If, that is, you can handle the truth.

The sad fact is that most players don't want to know the truth. They don't want to know how sloppy and self-indulgent their play can be. Can they really be that lazy? Or does a darker reason lurk?

WHY MOST PLAYERS DON'T KEEP BOOK

As in most fields of human endeavor, people playing poker tend to want the most they can possibly get for the least they can possibly do. Think about it: Would anybody study if they didn't have to? Would anybody spend time working on their game, refining their tools, if they didn't need that work and that refinement to close the gap between the performance they have and the performance they want? Of course not. Why bother?

And so it is that the typical Internet poker player has all these amazing statistical tools at his disposal and yet chooses to ignore them all. Having gotten into the lazy habits of live poker, where charts and graphs and stats and accounts of past performance are not available and not allowed, the lazy Internet player creates the same environment for himself at home. Though he *could* keep records, though he *could* keep book on his opponents, though he *could* use charts and graphs and stats and tables, he chooses instead to rely on the unaided capabilities of his own noggin. There in the moment, without the slightest benefit of back-up information, he makes ad hoc decisions about how to handle this game, these players, this hand, this bet, and so on.

Why? *For heaven's sake why?* Why has every online poker player not turned his home poker environment into a shrine for the study of poker? Why doesn't *everyone* build and maintain databases on themselves and on every online player who ever crosses their path? Maybe it's not laziness.

Maybe it's fear.

Suppose you do everything in your power to use the information streams that Internet poker offers. Suppose you track your own performance, your opponents' performance, optimum session hours, optimum game structures, and everything else, up to and including the harmonic convergence of favorable planets in the sky overhead.

Suppose you still sucked.

Suppose after all your efforts to improve your game, you remained the same weak, shoddy (here comes the hard word) *failure* you were before? How would that make you feel?

Awful. Awful unto the utmost.

So now here's the secret. Trying your hardest and failing is tougher on your ego than never trying at all. If you make *no effort* to improve your game, and the subsequent results don't please you, you have a handy rationale to fall back upon: *Well, this is really just a hobby for me. I don't have to try my best. Anyway, it's all luck anyhow.* If, however, you really commit yourself to bringing your online game to the highest level, and you still don't win, that's a crushing confrontation with failure.

Many people can't stomach that, so they take the easy way out. They use laziness to mask fear. No wonder they don't win. But it seems to me they're missing the point: it's process, not product that counts. If you try your best, you can draw emotional sustenance from trying your best, *even if you don't like the outcome.* For example: lifting weights builds muscle mass. How are you going to build up any muscle mass if you never, ever work out?

And even if the workout is a failure for some reason, at least the buildup goes on.

The buildup always goes on.

So I remind you again: *It ain't the doin', it's the tryin'.* If you don't give Internet poker your best effort (or even any poker your best effort) then you have no right to complain about your outcomes. But if you do give Internet poker your best effort (or even any poker your best effort) then the outcomes will take care of themselves.

That's easy to say, isn't it? *The outcomes will take care of themselves.* But they don't, not always. There you are with your charts and graphs all laid out before you. There you are, feverishly gathering and storing and using all the information you can get your hands on. There you are, having picked the right game at the right limits against the right opponents, and you still can't get past the lucky suck-out flopheads whose utter cluelessness seems to grow with their stack size. In these circumstances it's easy to feel like there's no point in working so hard for no benefit. It's easy to fall back on old habits: habits of laziness, fear, and ego protection.

Don't fall back! Keep working hard, and keep taking satisfaction in the hard work you do. They may take away your money—this time—but they can't take away your growth. And growth . . . grows. The more you have, the more you get.

That said—all of that said—I must warn you once again not to over-invest in data management. Don't allow yourself to become so distracted by data or so enamored of statistics that you neglect to play good, solid poker online. Remember that at any table, the player who influences your outcomes most is you. Don't go so far into data that you pass a point of diminishing returns.

Still, for the information *and* the analytical skill building that's in it, do yourself a favor, the biggest favor an online poker player can do: keep book. Keep track of your opponents and especially keep track of yourself, for keeping track of yourself is a marvelous way to keep yourself on track. Make your records full and complete and above all honest. Use your data not as a substitute for sensible play, but as an adjunct to your ever-advancing poker skills and awareness. Support your game with information. Handicap your foes. The more you handicap them, the less they handicap you.

7

THE DARK SIDE

Since the dawn of Internet poker, lo these handful of years ago, the word on everyone's lips has been . . . *cheating.* For fear of being cheated, some people won't go near the online game and regard with benign disdain the benighted fools who do. Are their fears realistic? Are collusion, nonrandom shuffles, and disappearing site operators a myth or a fact of Internet play?

Let's be realistic, it *is* possible to cheat online—just as it's possible to cheat in a real-world game. To imagine that cheating never happens is to imagine that teenagers never have sex or the government never lies; it's innocence to the point of ignorance. A healthy concern for your own self-interest is always a good thing, and since cheaters don't have your self-interest at heart, you'd do well to be on the lookout. Not so much on the lookout, however, that your healthy concern veers over into paranoia. If that happens, if you start seeing monsters under the proverbial online bed, you'll just end up skewing your play in a negative direction as a function of the fear you feel.

This is a lesson we learn in real-world games where we fear that collusion is taking place. We see a strange betting pattern, and it puts us on our guard. Smiley and Ed, we decide, are colluding by betting up the pot. So we become waranoid (wary to the point of paranoia) and make it a point not to get involved when Ed and Smiley join the pot. But it turns out that these two jamokes aren't partners; they're just crazy bad players who happen to be at the same table. By not mixing it up with them, we forsake the opportunity to take money from them both. If you fear you're being cheated, you should always leave the game, not necessarily because you're right but because, right or wrong, your fear will torque your play.

Just the other day, playing in a b&m cardroom, I got bet off a pot by a player who then *turned over his cards,* showing his pal his top set, and checking down the pot the rest of the way. This kind of soft-play cheating is, weirdly, a tolerated practice in most b&m cardrooms.

What could I do? If I stayed in the game with these guys, I'd be giving away two edges. First, I'd be letting them play partners at my expense. Second, I'd be so wound up in fury at the act that I'd leave my centered best game far behind. So instead, I did the only sensible thing. I left.

But there's a difference between leaving a game where there's evidence of cheating and never entering a game based solely on the fear of cheating. Let's explore the difference and see whether or not we can reach a reasonable middle ground.

COLLUSION

There are two possible types of collusion in both real-world and online poker: active collusion and passive collusion. Active collusion involves two or more players sharing information and artificially betting up a pot for the purpose of getting an innocent third party caught in the middle. Passive collusion involves just the exchange of information between and among cheating partners for the sake of skewing the odds in the cheaters' favor.

Active Collusion

You're playing hold'em at a full table that includes two wannabe wise guys named Wentzl and Droppler. You pick up something like A-T in middle position and take a flier on a cheap flop. Wentzl calls behind you, but Droppler raises, and it's called back around to you. You call the raise, figuring it likely that Wentzl will just call too. But Wentzl reraises, and Droppler pops him back. Now it's capped preflop, and you're not thrilled about paying four bets for this hand, but you throw your good money after bad.

What you don't know is that Wentzl and Droppler know each other's hands: Wentzl has pocket aces and Droppler has cheese. But Droppler doesn't care. He bets and raises at every opportunity, just as if he had a hand, or even a hand and a half. Poor you have unfortunately caught just enough of the flop to be on the hook—maybe something like top pair, top kicker. One could argue that all this betting should be a warning signal to you, but what the hell, they can't *both* have pocket aces, right?

If you were up against one legitimate foe, you could see the river for as little as two and a half big bets. But with Droppler working as Wentzl's stalking horse, you get caught in the middle of a raising war, the dreaded *whipsaw*, and find yourself spewing eight or ten bets into the pot.

And then . . . Droppler mucks! After all that betting, he folds on the river for a single bet, and you never get to see his cards. Wentzl rakes a huge pot, a pot made artificially large by the active collusion of these two players. Presumably they will meet later in the parking lot or the cyber parking lot and carve up their winnings.

Can you think of an instance in your poker career where you knew, or suspected, that your foes were shooting this angle? What were the circumstances? What tipped you off?

_____

_____

Passive Collusion

Passive collusion is active collusion without the whipsaw. To avoid being caught out in unusual betting patterns, passive colluders merely communicate their holdings to one another, in order to enhance each player's chances of winning by having more information about which cards are or are not in play.

Let's say that you and I are a couple of rogues playing seven-card stud online, and trying our hand at passive collusion. I'm holding (8-K) 3 (where the cards in parentheses are my hole cards) and you have (8-K) 8. I'm going to fold in any case, but you have a marginal call, *if* your cards are live. Because we're sharing information, you know that your cards aren't live, and you can fold with confidence. Next hand: I've got (K♣ Q♣) 9♣ and you've got (8♥ 5♦) 7♦. Thanks to passive collusion, I know that none of my clubs, straight cards, or pair cards are dead in your hand. This bends the deck a little more in my favor, and I can bet a little more aggressively, knowing that my cards are not just live but, in a sense, super-live.

How do we communicate our hands to each other? In the real world, we would use code. Maybe the way we stack our chips or hold our drinks indicates the rank and suit of our hidden holdings. Out here in cyberspace we don't bother

with code. We can use the phone. Or e-mail. Instant mes-
saging. We could be side by side on two computers. Hell,
we could be *the same guy* on two computers. How big an advantage is that?

Well, how big an advantage *is* that? One school of
thought contends that cheaters are generally such horrible
players to begin with that their own bad play neutralizes
any advantage they gain through the illicit exchange of information. It's also worth noting that just because Wentzl
has a big hand, his hand won't necessarily stand up. After
all, they know each other's cards, but they don't know *yours.*
Still, cheating is cheating; it's wrong in any form, and
whether it's hugely profitable, marginally profitable, or not
profitable at all, the cybercrooks should be hung by their
cybernecks until cyberdead. At the same time, I'm not
going to lie awake at night worrying about whether certain
foes are eking out an extra percent or two of edge by knowing each other's cards. My book on them both will tell me
whether they're winning players or not, and if they're generally winners, no matter how that's achieved, I'm going to
avoid them anyhow. You should do the same.

Can you think of a real-world poker game where you
caught, or thought you caught, other players flashing hand
strength signals to one another? How did it make you feel?

_____

_____

Your Response

If you think you've been the victim of active collusion online, you can always contact your online cardroom and ask
them to take steps. They will review the hand in question
and the hand histories of the players in question. They'll

examine how many times these two hook up in the same game and comb the records for suspicious betting patterns. If you think about it, you'll realize that such patterns are not hard to spot. After all, what's the point of having a whipsaw deal if you don't use it every chance you get?

Think about it a little longer, and you'll realize that, in at least one sense, it's easier to catch online cheaters than those in the b&m's. Sure they have the anonymity of the Internet to hide behind, and yes they may be conferenced into each other. But they've got to use this tool to make it pay, and the more they use it, the more likely a detectable pattern will emerge. Also, if someone cheats in a cardroom, the hand is over in a moment, and all the victim has is a nagging suspicion that *something's not quite kosher*. But if people cheat online they leave a trail behind. Every hand that's ever played on a site is recorded and stored. Software sorting tools can be used to measure betting patterns against known suspicious models. It won't be long before a site can tell the culprits, *"Hey you two, you can't play together"* or even *"you can't play at all."*

So what about passive collusion? Well, if it's a case of one player with more than one onscreen identity, this is fairly easy to detect. The online sites know your hometown and your IP address, and they can monitor the amount of time that two supposedly separate players spend at the same table. Correlating this information with unusual betting patterns, they can easily conclude that *you* are teamed up with *you*, freeze your assets, and shut you out of play.

Sure, it's possible that Weasel from Kiev meets Slimey from Fresno in a chatroom, and they make a deal to hook up for a little passive collusion. Their IP addresses are a world apart, and while they do seem to spend a lot of time at the same table, hey, maybe they just like each other's cyber company. In this case, the site has no technological means of divining Slimey and Weasel's evil purpose—but they do have the playing community to help them out. If enough people contact site support with the message that Slimey and Weasel don't smell right, it won't be long before Slimey and Weasel will be cut out, shut off, and hung by their cybernecks until cyberdead.

Which is not to say that collusion never happens, or that colluders are always caught. At any moment, two guys on the phone to each other—or six guys on a conference call—can work up a measurable edge against their unknowing opponents. One absolute protection against this is simply to play one-on-one. One foe can't collude with himself, and many online players, especially at higher limits, choose this option to protect themselves against people playing partners. If you go this route, though, you'd better be sure that your one-on-one skills are sharp, for a single skilled (honest) opponent can carve you up even more efficiently than a couple of inept angle-shooters.

Your other best defense against cheating is simply not to play for very high stakes. This protects you two ways: First, cheaters are less likely to operate at the lower limits where the chance for meaningful profit is limited. Second, if you should happen to be victimized, at least you won't be taken for much. This goes all the way back to our controlling idea about Internet poker: Don't play too large. Don't put much money into any game, so that if you lose it—even if you lose it to *cheaters*—you won't feel the need to slit your wrists.

RANDOM SHUFFLES AND CRACKED
ALGORITHMS

Every now and then you hear a cry of anguish echoing through cyberspace, a cry that sounds like this:

> *I was playing last night on www.pokeher.com when the following hand came up: Holding K-K, I raised under the gun, and everyone folded except the big blind, who flat-called. The flop came Q-J-T rainbow. I bet, he called. The turn was a seven. I bet, he called. The river was a deuce. I bet—he <u>raised</u>! I called, and lost to two pair, sevens and deuces. How could he possibly call me either before or after the flop? How could he even call me on the turn, knowing that he only had five outs to beat me, assuming that he wasn't already drawing dead to a straight or trips? <u>He must have known what cards were coming</u>! This freaking game is fixed!*

It's a common complaint, a common refrain: The game is fixed, the deck is iced, the shuffle is nonrandom, and some bright boys out there have cracked the algorithm to the point where they know what cards are coming off the deck. No wonder they make bad calls. They know they're a lock to win. What other possible explanation could there be?

How about this explanation? *They're just bad players!* If you took a beat like this in the real world, you wouldn't conclude that the player knew what cards were coming off the deck. You would conclude that she was a woodentop, doomed to lose. Well, online poker, being many players' entrée into the game, has a much higher proportion of woodentops, and yet some screaming waranoids believe that these innocent woodentops are not woodentops at all, but rather nefarious agents of evil—mysterious cyber pirates who have *cracked the algorithm* and now have a guaranteed license to steal.

Ever heard of Occam's Razor? It's a principle of logic that says, in essence, that the simplest explanation is likeliest to be true. Isaac Newton interpreted it this way: "We are to admit no more causes of natural things than such as are both true and sufficient to explain their appearances." Given a choice between your foe having cracked some alchemical algorithm on one hand, or just being a lucky dunderhead on the other hand, opt for the simplest solution: The dunderhead took the cheese. Deal with it, and move on.

Suppose you can't deal with it.

Suppose you need some reassurance that no one out there knows any more about the next outcome than you do? The sites will be happy to oblige, for almost every one posts information about how their decks are dealt. For the sake of making you feel comfortable playing in their games, they want you to know that their algorithms can't be cracked. They will happily explain (beyond most players' powers of comprehension) their use of shuffle algorithms, coupled with random number generators seeded from diversified non-predictable entropy pools, resulting in genuinely random decks whose outcomes cannot be predicted in any way from any available data. You can take this noise at face value or not as it suits your whim.

But just for comparison's sake, think about what a human dealer does in a real-world game. Maybe he scrambles the deck. Maybe he doesn't. He riffles the cards no more than three or four times, resulting in a redistribution of cards that can be called, at best, somewhat random. If he's careless, he exposes a card to the table as he cuts the deck before dealing. If he's really careless, he deals high, flashing

cards left and right, to the delight of any angle-shooter observant enough to scootch down low in his seat and catch
the action.

Real-world dealing in real-world games, then, is probably orders of magnitude less random and less secure than
what we see online. Yet concerns remain, precisely because
of what we *can't* see online. We can't see the cards being
scrambled, shuffled, and dealt, so we only have the site's
word for it that the deal is fair, true, and unpredictable. Nor
does it necessarily help that they dress up "their word" in
terms of shuffle algorithms and random number seeds.
Unless we're total math geeks, we just end up feeling inun-
dated by double talk, and more suspicious than ever. Perhaps it would be better if the sites just said, "Look, our deal
is random and fair; if you don't think so, don't play."

And that's my advice too: If you don't think so, don't
play, because, again, your own suspicion will move you off
your best game. You'll end up worrying so much about the
integrity of the shuffle that you'll forget to pay attention to
the way your opponents are playing. You'll get a bad beat
put on you and go on a special kind of tilt—the *this freaking
site is crooked* tilt. You won't play well. You will lose money.
Not because they cheat, but because you *fear* they do.

ALL-IN ANGLE SHOOTERS

One demonstrated area of online knavery is manipulation
of a site's all-in policy. As I've already noted, the sites take
steps to protect their players from technical glitches by
treating a disconnected player as all-in. For example, if you
and three other players have all put $20 into a pot and you
suddenly lose your Internet connection, the site will consider you all-in. You'll be eligible to win the $80 already in

the pot, but any further action will be on the side. Even if you have the best hand, you can only win what was in the pot before your connection went blooey.

But what if your connection didn't go blooey all by itself? What if you *made* it go blooey? And why in heaven's name would you do that? Let's look at a scenario.

You're playing pot-limit Omaha and find yourself, as is so often the case in pot-limit Omaha, with a big draw going up against a big hand. Your opponent makes a pot-size bet. You do a quick calculation and discover that you don't quite have the odds to justify a call. Common poker sense dictates that you lay down your hand, surrender the pot, and wait for a better situation. If you're an honest player this is exactly what you will do. But if you're a nefarious angle-shooter, you might consider a different option. You might pull the plug on your modem.

Back there at the game site, it looks like you've been disconnected, so the site software treats you as an all-in player. Now you have a freeroll for your big draw. If you get there, you win the money you've invested up to this point. If you miss, well, you don't lose any more money than you would have if you'd folded.

Yikes! Yow! What an angle! Why doesn't everyone shoot this angle all the time?

Well, they would if they could—at least the dishonest ones would. And so the sites have taken steps to prevent abuse of the all-in disconnect. It's called an all-in quota. If you receive all-in protection more than (depending on the site and the circumstances) one or two times per day, the site will treat you as having used up your all-in quota. Any subsequent disconnects within the next 24 hours will be treated as folded hands and not all-in situations.

This, then, is not an angle you can shoot a lot. And if you tried to shoot it on a regular basis, the site's fraud-sniffing software would perk up like a guard dog and say, "Hmm, well, it sure seems like Fuxxy's Internet connection goes bad a lot at strategically opportune times." Or the other players would rat you out. "Damn Fuxxy keeps going all-in on his fat draws!" Either way, you would find yourself barred from the site.

For honest players, it's a must that they keep track of their all-in disconnects. You only get one or two per day, and while you can always request that your all-in quota be reset, you're better off taking steps to ensure that your Internet connection is reliable and stable. Even if a disconnect results in all-in treatment and not a fold, who wants that to happen when you're sitting on a monster? And who wants to sit out the next 24 hours of action, for fear of it happening again, and this time costing you the whole pot?

It shouldn't have to be this way, of course. Honest players should not have to be penalized because angle shooters choose to exploit flaws in the system. "Well," as Groucho Marx wrote to his son, "that's life. As you journey through it, you will encounter all sorts of these nasty little upsets, and you will either learn to adjust to them or gradually go nuts."

THE ENEMY WITHIN

Beyond the fear that the sites are inadvertently leaving back doors open to shuffle pirates, there lurks a suspicion in some quarters that the sites themselves are the biggest crooks of all. Various scenarios of culpability have been suggested. Here's one: Bots.

Bots—short for robots—are poker-playing software disguised to look like real players on a given site. Presumably, these bots would be pre-programmed super-players guaranteed to win money for the house. Just one problem: the house is already guaranteed to win, thanks to the rake. The point of hosting the game is to keep the game going and keep the rake coming. For a site to add bots into the mix would be ultimately self defeating: if word got out, the site would be DOA.

I have found no evidence that bots are in use by any site now in operation. Well, one would hardly expect a site to admit to using bots, so the fact that they don't admit it doesn't mean it doesn't happen. Nor, however, should their denial be taken as a lie. With bots, as with all forms of suspected cheating, while a healthy skepticism is fine, the overly suspicious player is doomed to lose for other reasons.

You know, it's a funny thing about losing players. They're always looking for an external explanation for their bad outcomes. *The game is fixed. The site uses bots. I'm a victim of collusion.* Some people insist that the games must be fixed, or bot-populated, or *something* because so many players lose online. But as we've already discerned, in any raked game, *everyone* loses in the long run. The minority of superior players overcome this natural financial drain at the expense of the many inferior players. So—news flash—bad players lose. You don't need bots to explain this; Occam's Razor does just fine.

Now, there have been cases where the enemy within— the site itself—has definitely stolen money from the players, simply by vanishing from the face of the earth. I'm not going to name names for the very reason that I want *you* to do your homework before playing online. But keep in mind that there have been sites that turned out to be unwilling or unable to meet their cash-out obligations. They closed up shop and left their poor players holding the bag.

How can they get away with it?! cries the anguished player.

How can they collect my money and then not pay out when I want them to? How can they just simply steal off into the night? Here's how: Hosting an Internet poker site is not legal in the United States, so all the sites are offshore to begin with. If an Internet poker site takes the money and runs—and they're in, say, Turks and Cayucos—there's not a lot that anyone can do from a legal point of view.

If a new site comes along, maybe you're right not to trust it, for it could be a fly-by-night operation. Once a site has been around for a couple of years, and has established a record of stability and swift cash-outs, then I think you can afford to let down your guard a little. But with a new site, why not put in just a small amount of money and see how it goes? In this instance, as in all instances of Internet poker, limit your risk. Don't gamble more than you can stand to lose—to bots, bad-apple offshore operators, or anyone else. If you over-expose yourself and get victimized, you have no one to blame but yourself.

This sounds harsh, I know, but let's look at the situation from a slightly different perspective: Suppose you were playing at a b&m cardroom, and the dealer accidentally swept your (winning) cards into the muck. You'd stomp and shout, of course. But you'd also have to ask yourself if you had taken adequate steps to protect your hand. It's the first rule of cardroom poker, after all: players must protect their own hands.

The example is not analogous, I know. How, after all, can you "protect your hand" from a nefarious online site that just all of a sudden goes AWOL and turns up *error 404: file not found* one day? Well, you can't. But then again, if you were playing in a real-world game that got robbed at gunpoint, there wouldn't be much you could do—except plan not to play there again. You can't always protect your hand.

But you can always protect your interests.

There's a phrase for it in Latin: *caveat emptor;* let the buyer beware. If you play poker online, you expose yourself to all sorts of unique and possibly costly risks, the incredible disappearing poker site just one among them. I'm not saying that the lousy scoundrels should be allowed to take your money and run. But we already know that crap happens; this is just one more form of happening crap. Suck it up and deal, or, alternatively, deal yourself out.

Some people don't want to hear this. They want all the protections of a b&m cardroom (security guards and hidden cameras to name two) plus the convenience of 24/7 poker at home. And they want to be free to play for big money if they're so inclined. Fine, let 'em. But they'd do well to remember that reward doesn't come without risk.

In a perfect world, this sort of tragedy would never happen. Then again, in a perfect world, your sets would never get snapped off by inside straight draws and telemarketers would never call during dinner. If you're the victim of a foul play, by all means do everything you can to recoup your losses. The very best thing you can do (and I hate to keep flogging this beat equine, but it's really the bottom line) is make sure your losses aren't so heinous in the first place. Limit your risk. Limit. Limit.

I'm reminded of Reinhold Neibuhr's serenity prayer:

> *God grant me the serenity*
> *to accept the things I cannot change;*
> *courage to change the things I can;*
> *and wisdom to know the difference.*

Online poker requires a certain amount of serenity, courage, and wisdom. It does not require inordinate amounts of suspicion and paranoia. Yes, bad things happen—just as they do in real-world games. Take adequate steps to protect your interest, then set your worries aside and concentrate on playing your top game.

8

ONLINE PITFALLS

This chapter explores some of the traps that online players routinely fall into. If you have long experience online, you've probably already encountered some, most, or even all of these. If you're new to online poker, well, forewarned is forearmed.

OMHS

OMHS stands for "one more hand syndrome," and it's a particularly nefarious form of chair glue that afflicts online players. Chair glue, as we know, is the law of motion that states that a player at rest in a poker game tends to stay at rest unless acted upon by an outside force, such as the need to go to work or the fact of going broke. For many players in the real world, realities of their normal life act as a brake to their sessions. At some point, everyone goes home. But as we've already discussed, the online player doesn't have to go home—he's home already.

Thus a player at rest tends to stay at rest. Chair glue sticks him to his desk chair, and OMHS sets in. *One more lap,* he tells himself, *I'll just play through to my blinds.* Since the pace of play is so fast, we know that it won't take more than a few minutes to move us off the blinds, through the button, late position, middle position, early position, and back to the blinds again—when, we swear, we'll sign off and go to bed. Unless, alas, we decide to take just *one more lap* and set the whole cycle in motion again.

Online players get lost in a swamp of not knowing when to quit. Some resolve this problem by setting loss limits or win limits. They'll quit, they say, if they lose a hundred or win a hundred—or even get back to even. The fallacy of this strategy is well known: You don't leave a game because your stack reaches a certain size; you leave because the game's no good, or you're no good, or it's just freaking time to go. Planning to play until you win a certain amount or win your way back to even is just a rationalization for the fact that you *just can't quit.*

The problem in this context is not a gambling problem, it's a *playing* problem. Once upon a time I got hooked on a computer game called Lemmings, where the reward for finishing a level was the opportunity to tackle the next level. *One more level,* I told myself over and over again, *just one more level and then I'll quit.* Inevitable result: the hours flew by, carpal tunnel syndrome set in, and I didn't quit until I was literally too bleary eyed to see the screen. There was no money involved in this. I was just having fun, and I didn't want to stop.

It's fine to be having fun and not want to stop, but when money *is* involved, OMHS can lead to disastrous results. Players do get tired, and they do play worse when they become tired. When OMHS attacks, it steals not only your time but also your bankroll. Hey, I'm not saying that you can't win when you're stuck and tired—no, wait, yes I am. Quit! Quit now! You have to quit sometime!

Sure, fine, but how to organize an exit strategy? If *one more hand* doesn't work and *one more lap* doesn't work, and playing to a set chip limit is an irrelevant rationalization, how does anyone ever get out of a game? What is the magic force that breaks the bonds of chair glue and sets you free from online play?

Sadly, there is no magic. There's only discipline and common sense. Discipline means listening to the little voice inside your head that says, *"You know what? I'm not playing effectively anymore. I should stop."* Turn *I should stop* into *I shall stop* and you're home free. For my part, I have trained myself to respond automatically to the impulse to get up and go. Any time I hear even the faintest voice inside my head suggesting that I've had enough, I give tremendous credence to that voice. In other words, I let the *urge to quit* have veto power over any other thought. You can do the same. Just let *quit* mean *QUIT!* and *maybe quit soon* mean *QUIT!* and *one more lap around the table* mean *QUIT!* too.

Something else you might try is the simple strategy of setting an alarm clock. If you want to play for two hours, set that alarm for two hours, then respect the alarm when it rings. Many players find this strategy viable just because they're already trained to do what an alarm clock tells them to do: get up. Is it a trick? Yes. A shameless manipulation of you by you? Of course. But if it works—if it keeps you from yielding to the siren's song of *one more hand, one more lap*—then who cares whether it's a manipulation or not?

A variation of this strategy is to schedule your online session up against some other deadline. If you know that you absolutely, positively have to leave the house in an hour, then you can play for an hour knowing that OMHS can't grab you today. Ack, but what if it does?! What if you keep playing after the hour is over, to the point where you miss that important appointment or that rendezvous with friends or the movie you meant to go see? Then you have a problem that's neither a gambling problem nor a game-playing problem, but strictly a discipline problem. You have lost control over your decision-making capacity in one very important area: the decision whether to play poker or not. At that point, OMHS has morphed into a full-blown case of onlineitis, where you not only don't want to quit the game, you can no longer even detect the urge to do so. Don't beat yourself over the head if this happens—it's happened to most online players at one time or another. But *do* set an alarm, or configure some external means of motivating yourself out of the game. OMHS is the crippler of online bankrolls; don't let it cripple yours.

THE WANDERING MIND

Most players don't enter an online game already feeling understimulated. To the contrary, since poker is their passion and their love (or at least their hobby and their recreation) they go into the game fired up, psyched, committed to doing their best. With the best of intentions, they make book on all their foes and pay careful attention to the moves the other players all make. It isn't long before they start to feel like they've got the game "dialed in." They have a comfortable grasp on the play, the players, and the entire situation. They feel relaxed, at ease, at home.

That's when the mind wanders. That's when the busy brain starts looking around for *something else to do*. So what if Punchbuggy and Sylvia101 are doing battle in this hand? (a) You've already folded, and (b) you already have a tight read on both players. You won't learn anything new by following this action. You'll . . . just . . . be . . . bored. So you start playing with the paperclips on your desk, or bip over to check your e-mail, or maybe visit rec.gambling.poker to find out what the ranters have to say today. You don't have to worry about missing a hand, of course; the software will call you back to the game. So what if you missed Punchbuggy trying a hopeless bluff on the river and getting caught? It's probably not important.

And even if you *know* it's important, and *tell yourself* it's important, it's still hard to keep your mind on the game. As previously noted, there's so little input to go on. All you have is this one little piece of one little computer screen, occupying a modest percentage of your vision field, a tiny fraction of your hearing and none of your other senses at all. Real-world players are no strangers to complacency, but when the mind wanders in a cardroom, at least the player is still physically present. Minimize your picture of the game on your computer screen and it's *gone*. More precisely, you are gone; your head is out of the game.

One highly imperfect solution to this problem is one I've already discussed and dismissed: playing more than one game at the same time. *At least if I wander,* the mind rationalizes, *I'll be wandering to other poker. I will still be in the game.* Yes, true, but you're in the game for all the wrong reasons. You're not playing a second game to maximize your win rate (no matter how chimerical that goal may be). You're just playing that second game to minimize your boredom. But if one game isn't enough to occupy your mind, what makes you think two will do the trick? Maybe you need three. Four? Where does it end?

It ends where it began: deep inside you and your conscious state of mind. If you're serious about your winning, or even serious about your recreation, then you have to let this one activity be enough for you. Invest your mind in data mining. Ghost the other players in the game and try to predict their actions. Make little bets with yourself, even, about what the other players hold and who is likely to win. Let your mind wander . . . wander right back to the game. If you can do this—if you can let the play of a single online poker game fulfill your need to stay mentally engaged—then you have a decent shot at making the experience both profitable and pleasurable. But if you indulge in the urge to let your mind wander, not only will your poker be less than perfect, your enjoyment will go down too. Rather than being fun, online poker will just be frustrating, because it doesn't give you enough of what you need: stimulation.

It can, if you let it. It must, if you intend to show profit. The wandering mind takes money with it when it goes.

FESTE VORSTELLUNG

It's a small pitfall, hardly worth mentioning, but some sites deal your cards one at a time, and this can be a problem.

In the real world, when the dealer shoots your cards, it's up to you when and how you find out what they are. Savvy players wait not just until they have all their cards, but also until it's their turn to act before they look at their hand, to avoid giving away premature tells about whether they plan to call, raise, or fold. Premature tells are not an issue online, of course, since they cannot see your face or body, or get any advance indication of how you feel about your hand. Trouble is, *you* can get an advance indication of how you feel about your hand. Or more precisely, half your hand.

Many sites deal the cards out one at a time, so that there's maybe a second or two between the time you see each card. If that first card is good, you may find yourself rooting for the next card to be good, too. You want a strong hand or at least a playable one. If your first card is strong, you know you're halfway there. Now here comes the risk, the pitfall: left to its own devices, the subconscious mind will inflate the value of the second card, turning a folding holding into a marginal call and a marginal call into a raise. Your evaluation of your hand is torqued by your own desire for that hand to be strong.

Does this sort of thing actually happen? Can anticipation of a strong second card actually change your perception of that card's real strength? You may feel that you're above and beyond this sort of self-manipulation. You may, in fact, be right—but before you crow about your clarity of vision, may I introduce to you the concept of *feste vorstellung*?

Feste vorstellung is German for "fixed idea." A person's fixed idea is a cherished belief or deeply felt desire. A father, for example, may have the *feste vorstellung* that his son should be a baseball player, and he may hold onto this fixed idea despite firm evidence that his son can't run, hit, catch, or throw. The fixed idea, then, stands squarely between a person's perception and his outer reality, warping incoming information like a black hole bends gravity and light.

You're playing hold'em. In the moment between receiving an ace and getting your second card, a little *feste vorstellung* appears in the space between you and the computer screen. Laced with hope and desire, it anticipates receiving a second quality card, leading to a playable hand, *action*, and the promise of profit. Now here comes the second card. It's not an ace, it's an offsuit six, and your *feste vorstellung* pops like a balloon. But traces of it linger. For a moment—plenty of time to place a bet at the lightning speed of online play—that six looks better than it is, and that holding looks like a playable hand.

You need not fall victim to this pitfall. Just recognize its potential to affect you and a lot of its toxic power goes away. If you feel like you need to take extreme steps, simply look away from the screen until both your cards are dealt. Then you can evaluate them as a total holding, without your own phantom anticipation getting in the way.

It seems unfair that some sites deal the cards this way. I suspect that the choice was made by a software engineer and not a poker player. Be that as it may, the way the cards are dealt does differ from site to site. For example, www. truepoker.com deals your hole cards as hole cards. You actually have to click on them to see them. This opens the door to another tiny problem, one I'll discuss in the online tells section. For now, just pay attention to the way your favorite site deals your cards, and make sure that your own desire for a playable hand is not causing you to look at spam and see steak.

SHORTHANDED PLAY

Shorthanded play can be one of your most profitable opportunities in online poker, but it can also be a trouble spot, and you need to be aware of its special circumstances before you plunge on in.

Let's begin with the very urge to plunge. While many players gravitate toward shorthanded play to minimize the risk of collusion or to (notionally) maximize their profit potential, most players get involved for one simple reason: action. If you're playing shorthanded, you're constantly involved in the play of the game. In shorthanded hold'em, for example, you're either posting a blind or potentially attacking a blind on every single hand. Even if—gadzooks—you need to fold a hand, leaving your opponents heads-up, you know that the hand won't last long, no more than seconds, and then you'll be right back where you want to be . . . in action.

Online players don't necessarily start out as action junkies. They get into online poker with the avowed desire to enjoy the game and to apply their skills toward positive outcomes. But the pace of play, understimulation, and other factors previously discussed accumulate into what's called an addiction condition, a have-more-need-more circumstance in which the heightened level of online action creates within the player a tolerance for this heightened level of action and a subsequent desire for higher levels still. The faster you play, in other words, the faster you *can* play, and the faster you *want to* play, too. Faced, then, with the choice of a full game offering profit potential, or a short game offering action, action, action, many otherwise well-intentioned players jump right into the shorthanded fray.

Now the precise thing that got you into shorthanded play starts to work against you. The desire to be involved in action will cause you to loosen up your starting requirements or abandon them altogether. Against fewer opponents, you reason, you don't need such strong hands to compete anyway. Any cards are worth a call, and any half-decent hand is worth a raise. If you're specifically three-handed in hold'em or Omaha, the assault on the blinds becomes so commonplace that the raise itself is devalued and ultimately disregarded altogether. *Oh, you raised? And I've got 5-2? What the hell, I'll call your raise. And raise you back when it's your blind.*

So now you have this furious little maelstrom of raising with no thought to sensible play. Three shorthanded players motivated by the desire to be in action can easily work themselves into a betting frenzy. Three shorthanded players betting up the pot are each paying a proportionally higher rake (maybe three times higher) than they would at a full table. Three shorthanded players going nuts on each other drag each other down by equal degrees.

What should you do to avoid this pitfall? Should you ignore shorthanded play altogether? Of course not. Sometimes, shorthanded games are the only ones available; frequently these games are ripe targets of opportunity. But to make the most of these opportunities, there are three things you must do.

1. *Get your mind right.* Make sure you are entering the shorthanded fray for the sake of winning money and not just to meet your need for speed. Be *very clear* about this, for it's easy to delude yourself into thinking that you're seeking profit, when it's really only buzz.

2. *Got book?* Let your data management skills help you select shorthanded games in which you have a definite advantage. Remember, if players are equally skilled, no one but the house will win. You must be *better* than your foes to thrive shorthanded, and you can be confident that you *are* better if you've got good book.

3. *Evade the clueless parade.* In shorthanded games online, everyone seems to sink to the same level of loose calls and promiscuous raises. If you do nothing but maintain appropriate selective aggressiveness—playing marginally tighter and marginally stronger than the other players—you can do quite well.

PREDATION

Like shorthanded play, one-on-one games can be highly profitable under the right circumstances. Under the *wrong* circumstances, though, they can be a real stroll through a minefield.

As with shorthanded play, you need to monitor your motivation for playing heads-up. Some players stick to heads-up play because it absolutely eliminates the threat of collusion. Others consider themselves (rightly or wrongly) to be superior players and seek to make the most of their skill differential in the heads-up pressure cooker. But the rest—most—are just in it for the action. Playing heads-up they know they're *never* not involved, and that is the specific allure. If it's the specific allure to you, I suggest you give your rationale a cold, hard look. You may be in the right game for the wrong reason, and that's a recipe for mayhem.

Recognizing that many skilled and conscientious online players are keeping thorough book on their foes, you can't disregard the possibility of running into an online predator or shark. These players are making the very most of their online opportunities by looking specifically for opportunities to isolate opponents whom they know they can beat. If you're going to go one-on-one against anybody, you'd damn well better have book on them, because they may very well have book on you.

Predators seek nothing less than the total annihilation of your stack. They want your money, and they want it fast, because they know that the rake will take its toll over time: if they play you even, or even close to even, you'll both lose, and while predators don't care if *you* lose, they sure don't want to see *themselves* lose. That's why you'll see this sort of player coming at you super-aggressively. He wants to build pots, and he wants to put you on tilt. He knows that if he can get you leaning the wrong way, he can take you for everything you've got.

You'll know you're up against a predator when you find yourself playing someone who raises almost constantly and who never backs down. He's looking for the slightest hint of fear or passivity in your play and seeks to find this flaw through the application of extreme pressure. He wants to put himself in the position where he can beat you by browbeating you, by betting you off your hand and by making you afraid to use the same tactics back. He reasons that you'll try to beat him by trapping and drawing out— catching lucky, in other words. And he knows what every solid predator knows: if you have to catch lucky to win, you *can't* win, not one-on-one against a skilled opponent.

Are there really players out there so strong and fearless and skillful that they can victimize the weak—or even the solid and sensible—in this way? Of course there are! In a perfect world, *you are that player,* but if you find yourself up against someone you can't beat, it's imperative that you stay out of his way. Don't let your big ego get you into big trouble. Respect the fact that some players are better than others and some players are better than you.

Don't challenge strong players; challenge weak ones. That's what they're there for.

But how can you know for sure? Absent prior book on your foe, how can you know whether you're having a friendly little one-on-one joust or setting yourself up to be fish food? Don't wonder; find out: play very carefully at first. Don't be aggressive and don't be tricky. Play solid, straightforward poker and let your foe reveal his skills and abilities to you. If you come to believe you can outthink him or dominate him, then map out a strategy to do so. But if you get the sense that you're being *played,* if you find that your foe has you consistently guessing wrong, or even just playing reactive rather than proactive poker, get the heck out now! Don't give him a chance to mook you for all your chips. Leave! Leave now! Why wouldn't you?

Well, *why* wouldn't you? It may be that you've passed the point of pain. By the time you realize you're in trouble, you may have already lost so much money to this aggravating foe that nothing matters now but winback or payback. It may also be an ego issue: you don't want to give this player the satisfaction of seeing you back down.

I'd rather give him satisfaction than money, but that's just me.

So let's say you come to your senses, engage in damage control, and leave the game. Your problems are over, right? Not necessarily. Having tasted blood, this particular shark may decide to follow you around. There's an equivalent behavior in online role-playing games, where certain aggressive players called *griefers* follow unsuspecting opponents (especially newbies) around an online role-playing game site for the express purpose of making their online lives hell. The poker predator doesn't want to make you suffer, per se; he just wants your money, and if he thinks that following you from game to game will accomplish that goal, expect to see his smiling cyberface everywhere you go.

If you see a certain player jumping from the game you just left to the game you've just joined, you'd better beware: He thinks he has a significant advantage over you. And he might, too, because a player who thinks he has your number is bound to play more confidently and aggressively, and thus perform better, against you.

And thus reinforce his opinion that your money is there for the taking.

If he has this opinion in the real world, he might be blocked from acting upon it by the number of open seats at various tables and the floor manager's efforts to keep all her games balanced and full. Online, this is not a problem. If he wants to follow you he'll follow you, and there's nothing you can do about it, short of swallowing your pride and logging off.

Remember your Shakespeare: "The better part of valor is discretion." Better yet, consider the quote in context: *Henry IV, Part 1,* act V, scene IV; Falstaff has just saved his own life by feigning death. He gets up and says,

> *To die is to be a counterfeit; for he is but the counterfeit of a man who hath not the life of a man: but to counterfeit dying, when a man thereby liveth, is to be no counterfeit, but the true and perfect image of life indeed. The better part of valor is discretion; in the which better part I have saved my life.*

Feign death if you have to. Allow yourself to look like a coward if that's what it takes to avert disaster. The Internet is filled with scrappy foes. You'll be far better than some and far worse than others. There's no shame in admitting that an opponent has your number. The only shame comes in knowing this thing and letting him "predate" you just the same.

Be the bully, especially one-on-one, or don't be involved at all.

UNDERESTIMATING THE UNSEEN THREAT

You're playing online poker and find yourself contesting against a certain DaisyMae from Knoxville. Based on her name, you assume she's a woman. Based on your knowledge of geography, you assume she's from Tennessee. You know they don't play legal poker in Tennessee, so you further assume that she has neither long experience nor, probably, superior skills in poker.

Then, being a conscientious Killer Poker player, you go back and challenge all of the assumptions you just made. Just because she *calls* herself DaisyMae, that's not necessarily her real name—nor even her real gender. Just because she claims Knoxville as her home (and types, "Nice hand, ya'll" in the chat window) doesn't necessarily mean she's telling the truth—nor even that the Knoxville she putatively comes from is the one in Tennessee. And even if these two points are true points defining a line, there's no guarantee that the line leads to the conclusion DaisyMae can't play.

So you're wary. You don't credit DaisyMae with extraordinary skill, but on the other hand you don't assume that the image she projects is a real one. You vow not to be taken in by her nickname or hometown or chosen avatar or chat.

If you were playing against her in a cardroom, you could read her capability in her face and body. You could measure her focus and her discipline from the way she looks at her cards, places her bets, watches the action after she folds, and a dozen other verbal and nonverbal cues. You might be totally wrong in your judgment, but this would be an error of analysis, not assumptions. Since you're facing her in cyberspace, you have less direct information to draw upon. Having discounted her name and locale and line of chat, you can only deduce the quality of her play from available evidence. You can only gauge her performance by the hands she plays and the cards she shows. You can't know enough, at least at first, to give her the respect, and maybe even the wide berth, she might ultimately prove to deserve.

While you exist in ignorance of her real ability, you run

the risk of underestimating her. Why? *Because you can't see her!* She is an unseen threat, and the unseen threat can seem to be no real threat at all.

Good players, strong players, have to guard against the natural tendency to underestimate their opponents anyway. It's an easy mistake to make, when confidence veers over into arrogance, and it's especially easy to make this mistake online, where you can't look into your opponents' eyes and see, unmistakably, that they have the better of you. So it is that with a certain amount of hubris a certain sort of player takes a seat in an online game and concludes, without any real evidence to support the assertion, that *these chumps are all losers and they will give their money to me!*

You raise with A-A, and DaisyMae calls. *Idiot! Doesn't she know I have pocket aces?* No, she doesn't know you have pocket aces—that's why she called. Knowing what you know about your hand, and simultaneously not knowing anything about DaisyMae, you conclude that she is a maker of mistakes. What do we do with mistake makers? Attack, of course; punish! Force them into situations where they're making bad decisions. We know that we'll make money in the long run if our ability to make decisions is materially better than theirs.

If.

An assumption—a hidden and untested *if*—has crept into your thinking here. Believing yourself to be a strong player, you naturally believe your foes to be generally inferior to you. You naturally believe that your strong-arm tactics will work, that your opponents are too thick-headed to adjust, and that sooner or later (probably sooner, you figure) the sheep will be shorn.

These beliefs may be perfectly valid, but then again they may not. And in the early stages of an online poker session, it's very difficult to accumulate hard evidence one way or another. Did that player call because he's clueless or because he computed the odds and concluded that the pot had his draw covered? You don't know. In the real world you could maybe watch his face and correlate the faraway look with a pot-odds calculation. In cyberspace . . . well . . . he paused before he bet, but was he calculating odds or just running to the fridge for a soda?

In real-world poker, people will try to lead you astray with their image. They'll act strong when they're weak, act daft when they're savvy, and so on. In the cyberspace game, *you lead yourself astray.* The combination of limited insight into your opponents' and your own (even well-intentioned) confidence can lead you to conclude that you have an edge when, in fact, you don't.

How can you avoid this pitfall? Part of the answer is by now well known to you: have book. Know your opponents based on their past performance, and really *know* whether they're good players or just chuckleheaded luckyboys. Beyond that, take the time in your online session to *go slow and learn.* Play very tight to start, and watch your foes closely. Determine who's tricky and who's not. Determine who's strong and aggressive versus passive and weak. Make first-order classifications of all your foes, then update those classifications as they reveal new information about the way they play. At minimum, divide them into the categories of *better than me, equal to me* or *worse than me.* In this way, at minimum, you'll know whom to attack and whom to avoid.

The fact is that you will not know your foes at first. It will take a lot of hands to figure out how good they really are, many more hands, in fact, than in the real world, because you have so little hard evidence to go on and so must rely on deduction and inference developed over time. This argues strongly for planning your online sessions carefully, and for making sure that you have enough time to do it right. Your effort here resembles detective work. Always give yourself enough time and tools to crack the case.

Poker is patience; this we know. Based on our b&m experience, we're well acquainted with the need to wait for the right cards and the right situation. Online, we must wait for something else: we must wait for our opponents to reveal their true nature. Be patient with this, and be respectful of the unseen threat. Don't assume going in that they're all woodentops. They may very well be—but give them a chance to prove it.

RUDENESS AS AN INTERNET WEAPON

Poker players can be *so* rude. In the real world, intolerable airholes pollute the atmosphere of the game with tossed cards and hurled invective, with snide comments about other people's play or the dealer's ancestry, with incessant requests for deck changes, or with interminable cell phone conversations. Some of us, alas, have occasionally *been* such airholes, but perhaps we can be forgiven the odd momentary loss of temper brought on by one too many ugly suckouts. We are not the sort of players who would be intentionally and premeditatedly rude just to tick off our opponents and put the bastards on tilt.

These tactically rude players do exist, though. They exist in every cardroom, and online cardrooms are no exception. Granted, they can't throw drinks or blow smoke in your face, but there are a few ways that Internet poker players can be ill behaved, and in defense against these players, we need to watch out for such displays and know how to respond.

The most obvious way for a player to be rude is to use

the chat box or chat window to needle you and try to get under your skin. What would you make, for example, of a predator who *announced* his intention to rip your flesh? It could happen, you know, for sound strategic reasons.

You've just had your stack halved in a $10–$20 hold'em game by a strong player named Polonius. Rather than give him all your money, and the attendant satisfaction of busting you, you have beaten a strategic retreat to a $5–$10 Omaha/8 game on the same site. You're enjoying a few minutes of tranquil success, when suddenly here comes Polonius, taking a seat in the game. You think it may be coincidence—perhaps he's just looking for greener pastures—but then this line of chat appears:

Hey, FuzzyBunny101, I thought you went to bed.

You ignore him. Even though your screen name is Fuzzy-Bunny101, and so there's very little chance that he's talking to anyone but you, you'd just as soon not get involved. But then he types something else. Maybe he won't be so overt as to call you a coward to your face. Maybe he'll just say:

Guess I was too much for you, huh? Or do you just
prefer Omaha?

You don't dignify his taunt with a response. But he doesn't let up. He issues a challenge instead.

How 'bout a little one-on-one? Why not meet me in the
Blue Velvet Room?

What he wants, obviously, is to get you alone so that he can carve you up by himself. Even if you don't fall for this ploy, Polonius doesn't mind, because the rest of the table gets to see him talking smack, and he thus establishes himself as a bully without ever having played a hand. Watching him taunt you, the rest of the table becomes scared or annoyed or angry or resentful or some combination of all. It may even be that some lesser mind will take up the challenge and go off to play Polonius heads-up.

And Polonius might even lose, but probably not, because he has such a strong psychological edge going in.

Does this sort of rude chat actually take place online? Of course it does, and for the obvious reason that no one has to worry about you getting mad enough to take a poke at them. They *want* you that mad. They want you to take the only poke you *can* take. They want you to try and punish them with bets. Do it, and they've got you right where they want you: on tilt, or if not completely on tilt, at least thinking about them when you should be thinking about you.

How can you defend against this noise? You can always ignore it, and if you find you can't ignore it, you can always turn it off. Every site gives you the option of either turning off all players' chat or selectively filtering voices you don't want to hear. There's something satisfying in thinking about a player thinking he's chatting at you, and you don't even know it. It's like covering your ears and saying, "I can't hear you!"

You might try chatting back, responding not in kind but in kindness, demonstrating that your loudmouth foe can't get a rise out of you. While I'm inclined to go that route—being a writer, I figure I can chat rings around most anyone—I don't recommend it. Why give even the vaguest impression that you're buying into his game? Stay mum. Play strong, solid poker, and let the chatter's written words fall on blind eyes.

FuzzyBunny101? Are you there, pal? Come in Fuzz,
Earth to Fuzz . . .

Eventually he'll get bored, or shouted down by the other players.

Or ratted out.

In the early days of Internet poker, chat was pretty much unregulated. A player could be as offensive as she liked and no one tried to stop her. These days, almost every site has rules against rude or abusive chat. If Polonius goes too far, he'll be shut out of the site, and then he'll just have to take his loud mouth elsewhere. When in doubt, rat him out.

The other form of rudeness one typically sees on the Internet is dawdly play. Players can make their decisions in an instant online and when a player takes more than an instant, say 10 or 15 seconds or more, it can seem like an epoch. It can decidedly cheese off those foes who have gotten used to, maybe even grown dependent on, the accelerated pace of play. If a player drags the pace of the game down too much, she'll definitely hear about it from the other players.

Some few players, then, will stall on purpose, in hopes that it makes you impatient. They figure the more impatient you become, the less perfectly you will play. As with the aggressive chatter, don't bother responding. If you urge this jerk to play faster, you just give him the satisfaction of knowing he's gotten under your skin.

Overt rudeness, especially for tactical reasons, is becoming increasingly rare online. In many respects, sites are more diligent about policing this crap than their b&m counterparts. But it's still up to you to protect your own interests. Your first best defense is to just ignore rudeness. If it's really annoying, change games or change sites. If it's annoying *and* relentless, report it to the powers-that-be. That's not so satisfying as taking a poke at the player, but it does get the job done.

CONSCIOUSNESS ABUSE

In his marvelous book, *Play Poker, Quit Work and Sleep Till Noon* (published in 1977 by Bacchus Press) John Fox wrote the definitive word on alcohol and poker:

> *If you are a **very** bad player to start with, drinking probably won't hurt your game too much. For **anyone** else, one drink is too much, two drinks are ridiculous.*

In the real world, where driving to and from the cardroom is part of most players' experience, the dangers of drinking and driving are sufficient reason for most to keep their chips and spirits separate. Online, however, in the privacy of your own home, it's a different matter. Many is the player who has decided to enhance his online playing experience with a glass of fine wine, rubbed scotch, or malt beverage. These players don't have to worry about driving home, so they can go nuts with their libations, and nothing suffers but the quality of their play.

Look, I'm not here to tell you that you have to be a teetotaler to play poker online. You're free to do what you want. Again, make sure you have clarity about your goals. If you want to have a poker party, and booze helps that, then go ahead and drink. Just don't imagine it will improve your outcomes or your bottom line.

Some—shall we say—grain enthusiasts insist that the drinker hurts himself less in the online environment than in the b&m's. These player/quaffers point out that their foes can't see them drink and so don't have any idea what straight or altered state they're in. Nor do they leave themselves vulnerable to attack from opponents savvy enough to target the alcohol-impaired. This is all true, of course, but it ignores the obvious point that drinkers are their own worst enemies. Forget about how others may victimize you— how will you victimize yourself? Will you loosen up your starting requirements, forget to pay attention to folded cards, try to run your bluffs on booze-fueled bravado alone? Success in poker stands on such a thin margin to begin with. How good would you have to be to overcome the handicap that booze-clouded thinking would bring?

You want to be handicapped, fine, be handicapped. Just don't cry in your beer when your decision-making skills go in the toilet and your game falls apart.

Nor is alcohol the only chemical that can move a player out of her productive playing zone and into the twilight zone instead. Remember what I said earlier about online poker requiring that you enter an effective resource state? It's axiomatic that no mind-altering substance—pot, pills, whatever—can do anything but degrade the quality of this state.

For that matter, you can be 100 percent clean and sober and still be 100 percent off your game. Let's say you were sick, you had the flu. The bad news is you're too sick to go to work. The good news is you're not too sick to prop yourself up in front of your computer. Hell, maybe you can even pull a laptop into bed with you. You could spend all the hours of your convalescence playing online poker. Wouldn't that be heaven?

Sure it would.

Either that or hell.

How well do you imagine you can play in your fevered state? You'd never drag yourself to a card club in that condition. If you're not feeling your best—if you're not sharp, clear-eyed, hale, and healthy—you play poker at your peril. You *will* make mistakes. You *will* lose money. Why give yourself that grief?

Okay, you're clean, sober, *and* healthy. You're home free, right?

Don't forget that you can start out feeling perfectly mentally centered, and yet descend over time into a mental fog. It's called *getting tired,* and it happens to every player who logs enough hours. The real trouble with playing tired is that you're often so tired you don't know how tired you are, and you can't even make the sensible decision to quit. This is a situation called *oxygen-debt stupidity,* a problem reinforced by the online environment, where your schedule is your own, going home is not an issue, and the game never breaks.

Can you think of any other ways that a player could degrade his or her consciousness? Do you dare to name ways you abuse yours?

_____

_____

What about loud music? Watching TV? Talking on the phone? Will these self-induced distractions not also impede concentration?

Internet poker is all about free will. Every online poker player is free (within reason) to play the game as he or she sees fit. You want to play naked? Go ahead. You could never do that in a b&m. Want to scream at the screen, curse your foes for their bonehead plays? You can do that, too, and venting your frustration may even keep you on an even keel. If you so choose, your cardroom is *never* non-smoking. By extension, if you want to drink or smoke or whatever while you play, that's your choice, and no one will suffer the consequences but you.

I have spoken in general terms about general pitfalls, and I hope they serve as useful warnings for your own play. They won't be nearly so useful, though, as the warnings you post to yourself. So think about areas where you are at risk, and see if you can generate a list of online pitfalls particular to your skill level, style of play, or atavistic indulgences.

_____

_____

It's useful reading about pitfalls; it's twice as useful acquainting yourself with ones of your own.

9

WINNING TACTICS FOR
ONLINE PLAY

Just as online play has its own unique set of pitfalls, it also
has distinctive opportunities that the savvy online player
can routinely exploit. Above and beyond your normal solid
game of Killer Poker, there are things you can do online—
things you can't do in the real world—to maximize your
edge. This chapter examines some of the large and small
advantages you can accrue.

FINDING THE FISH IS JOB ONE

While it's true that the sharp b&m player goes looking for
soft tables and weak opponents, the constrictions of the
real-world game often prevent him from fully exploiting
the fish he spots. Sign-up boards are his foe. He may have
located some juicy targets in one of three or four $10–$20
hold'em games, but when his name gets to the top of the
list, he might not get a seat in his game of choice. Sure, he
can put in for a table change, but there's no guarantee that
he'll get moved even then to the table he wants. What if
the best game is the main game, but our hero is stuck in

must-move limbo? Maybe the house is determined to keep a balanced number of players per table, so that the floorman's desire for balance thwarts the player's desire to exploit weak foes. In all cases, time is passing, and the game is going on and the fish are getting away.

An online player doesn't face these obstacles. If you want to find a fish, all you have to do is visit the lobby of your favorite online site and cross-reference the names of the players you find there against your list of known weakies and wallies. In the worst case, the players you want to attack are already in a full game. So you put your name on the waiting list for that game, and go off hunting for other opportunities.

This ability to put your name on waiting lists for specific games is a tremendous advantage to those who use the tool. With good book on your foes, and a little homework and patience on your part, you need never sit in on anything less than an excellent game. Nor is your use of this tool limited to one site. If you have money in play at several sites, you can be prospecting among them for the weakest foes. Imagine being able to scout out games at the Bellagio and the Mirage—and Commerce and the Bike, plus clubs in Mississippi and New Jersey, the Aviation Club France and Casino Baden—all at the same time. You'd have to be entirely unobservant or inexcusably lazy not to profit from such a situation.

And yet, players fail every day to profit from this very situation online. They grab for the first seat in the first game available at their limit. Once settled into that seat, they never look around for alternatives. They never "crane their necks," so to speak, to see if the next table over offers a better prospect. Some players' tunnel vision takes them straight to the shortest-handed game, the siren's song of *action, action, action* calling them in. Hey, if you want action, fine, cast yourself upon those rocks. But if you want profit, it pays to shop around.

Here's where your book becomes indispensable. In order to make informed choices, you have to be, well, informed. Your ability to link your choice of games to the presence of *known beatable foes* guarantees that there will always be at least *someone* you dominate. Stand above them and throw rocks. That's what winning poker is all about.

Real-world players have this option too, of course. Walking into their regular club, they can tell at a glance where the fish are schooling and, conversely, where the sharks all lurk. The thing is, though, their depth of understanding may go no deeper than *fish* and *shark*. Even if they keep book on their foes, it's likely to be mental book, not written book, and neither so detailed nor reliable as its online equivalent. You, on the other hand, with your detailed and comprehensive notebooks or spreadsheets, are able to identify not just *which* foes can be exploited, but *how* they can be exploited.

Consider: You're shopping the sign-up lists, and you notice a player whose name, Penny Poker, rings a bell. Consulting your book, you discover that Penny is a consistent loser at her normal game and limit: $5–$10 hold'em. But today you find her in the strange new world of Omaha/8—and not just Omaha/8 but $20–$40 O/8 at that! Assuming you have the bankroll to back your play, you'll definitely want to go after this player, for your book verifies that she's outside her zone of comfort in two important ways, playing a game she does not normally play and playing at a much higher limit than usual.

Use the lists. *Use* your book. Make the most of the opportunity that the online sites hand you every day for free. There's a saying in poker, "Don't leave money lying on the table." In other words, if it's there to be won, *win it!*

Most players won't, you know. Most players are too lazy or arrogant or action-starved to do anything at all except leap into the fray. These players become targets of a different sort, but for now just pity them (and thank them) for overlooking the free money lying on the table. And again, ask yourself why you're here. If you like money, a bit of looking around and a bit of thoughtful research can put you in a position to win far more than your share.

ADVANCED STRATEGIES FOR FINDING THE FISH

Ever played in a b&m casino that offers a big, fat jackpot? If so, I'm sure you've noticed that some (exceptionally bad) players are playing there just in the hope of hitting that jackpot. Being not very good players to begin with, and with their judgment further skewed by jackpot fever, they present themselves as choice morsels to strong talented players—players who don't give a fig about jackpots, but love to munch up on the jackpot-heads. Thus you find the natural geographic procession of good players going where the bad players are. It's called following the fish, and it happens on the Internet in spades.

To follow the fish, you have to think like them and anticipate where they will go. Some strong players pursuing this strategy tend to make their way to the biggest Internet poker sites, or the ones that advertise most, using the logic that new players, with nothing better to go on, will naturally gravitate to the most well-known online games. To use this strategy effectively, simply study the poker magazines (like *Card Player*) and especially the *non-poker* gaming magazines (like *Casino Player*) and see which sites are advertising the most or generating the most buzz. It's especially important to check out the general interest gaming publications, because they're advertising to *cross-over gamblers,* people whose interest in online poker will, at least at first, far outstrip their abilities.

While doing this homework (not forgetting to visit such online poker information sites as www.pokerpages.com and the venerable rec.gambling.poker) make sure to keep a weather eye peeled for brand new sites. At the time of this writing, I was able to identify upwards of 25 online poker sites. And that number grows larger every day. Lately I've seen come-ons touting them as a business opportunity: *"Own your own online poker cardroom today!"* Far be it from me to judge the relative merits of this (okay, I'll say it, highly dubious) business opportunity, but the fact of this come-on points out a *clear opportunity* for Killer Poker players like you. Every new site must do something to call attention to itself. Their promotional efforts generally fall into three categories, each having a particular allure to new players:

1. *They advertise outside of normal poker channels.* Knowing that at least part of their business must come from beyond the existing player base, new sites tend to extend their message to new players.

2. *They offer hefty sign-up bonuses.* Again, knowing that their success is critical to building and sustaining games, they'll usually pay dollar bonuses to players who come to, and stay in, their real-money games. Everybody loves a bargain; new players are no exception.

3. *They have big jackpots.* And jackpots draw jackpot-heads, who are generally well below the mean in terms of poker expertise.

The math of it, then, is childishly simple: New site + new players = $$ 4 U.

Hey, while we're talking math, let's throw in a little algebra. I draw your attention to the following graph:

Money-making opportunities at new online poker sites

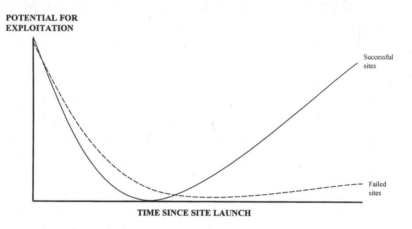

When a site is new, brand new, it attracts the highest proportion of new players, people susceptible to advertising, bonus promotions, promises of jackpots or all of the above. Over time, a natural shakeout occurs, as sites resolve themselves into the respective categories of "successful" and "failed." In both cases, the initial rush of new money tapers off (because the worst of the new players bust out and go home) and the profit potential for skilled players begins to bottom out. If the site has quality—good promotion, good functionality, and good support—it can grow a viable player base and continue on as a profitable playing opportunity. If the site lacks quality, it fails to keep a critical mass of players and sinks down to the low-interest, low-traffic end of the pool. Bad players don't come to the site because they don't know about it or don't like it. Good players don't come to the site because the bad players don't.

The savvy shark is thus always keeping book not just on the players but on the sites themselves and using her analysis of them to determine whether a given site is fresh or fading. Remember that it's not merely a matter of raw traffic to a site, but the specific makeup of the players who comprise that traffic. You can go to the gigantic online sites and your prospects will be limited by the inordinate number of other sharks swimming in the same waters. Alternatively, you can go to a nearly dormant site, a backwater, so to speak, where there are damn few fish—but also no competing sharks.

In poker, game selection is everything. In online poker, game selection starts with site selection, and goes forward from there. If you play at the same site every day because it's "your favorite" or it's "the best" you're guaranteed to be missing at least an equal opportunity elsewhere. Above all, it should be your practice to sample every new site that comes along. The early shark gets the fish.

THE STRENGTH OF STRAIGHTFORWARD PLAY

In his book, *Fundamental Secrets of Poker,* Mike Caro warns skilled players against something called "fancy play syndrome," the tendency of the talented few to want to show off their skills for people who, alas, just aren't paying attention. There's no point in bluffing for advertising purposes, for example, if the people you're bluffing into are oblivious to advertising and making no effort to go to school on your play.

FPS, according to Caro, is most likely to be found at low-limit games, because low-limit players are more likely to be, well, clueless. My experience of the online game suggests that this anti-FPS stance should be extended to the middle limits as online games typically have more clueless players playing higher. In harmony with your strategy of following the fish, if you find yourself in a game where fancy plays would work, well, not to put too fine a point on it, *you're in the wrong game*. No matter how clever a player you are, you'll simply make more money exploiting bad players with straightforward play than challenging skilled players with tricky moves.

Some students of the online game recommend never bluffing. They make the case—and I think it's a solid one—that simply waiting for good cards and then betting the beejeezus out of them is, in and of itself, a sufficiently profitable strategy. Since most online players call too much, it only makes sense to exploit their flaw by pushing your good hands and throwing the rest away.

This assumes, of course, that the game is not so relentlessly passive that bets are there for the thieving. You *will* find games like this, and should adjust your play accordingly. But I promise you this: if you come out raising with cheese hands, you might be able to steal a blind or two for a hand or two, but pretty soon your opponents will get tired of folding (they're there for the action, remember) and even the most tight/passive of players will start calling your raises, because your raises will have lost all currency. Then you'll find yourself in the situation of pushing inferior hands, and that's no way to make money. Best bet: Just wait for good cards. Wait, and push.

This strategy further assumes that you can resist the carny bark of *action, action, action*. It's easy to play selectively aggressively in the b&m environment. Your interest in watching other players, your desire to keep the respect of your peers, and the fact that the chips and money seem so much more real all conspire to keep you on the straight and narrow. Online, *everyone* has trouble holding their discipline. If you can hold yours, then your selective/aggressive strategy of *when you get the goods, bet the goods,* is bound to work out well.

Obviously if your book has identified certain players as ones who can be pushed off a pot, by all means go ahead and push them, no matter what cards you hold. Just don't assume that the majority of your foes are this timid and scared. In the main, yes, they are timid and scared *but they'll call anyway.* That's fine. We like it when they call too much. No further action is required on our part than appropriately selective/aggressive poker.

Again—and this point simply cannot be stressed enough—if you find yourself in a game where selective/aggressive Killer Poker won't get the job done, *just get out.* There is always a profitable game out there somewhere on the Internet. You may have to hunt for it, or you may have to wait a little while and check back later, but if you're not in a game that you can beat, you're simply not doing your homework.

It's not true that the online playing community is universally clueless; it *is* true that the online playing community is so abundantly populated with clueless players that the savvy player need never mix with any other kind.

BALLISITIC BULLY (WITH HAPPY CHAT)

Good players can grind out reasonable wins online. Expert players should expect their net profit to be higher online than in the b&ms if for no other reason than they don't have to tip, so that's a dollar or two from every pot they win that *stays* in the pot they win. They likewise neither have to pay a premium for food or drink, nor cover their own overhead of gasoline or valet parking or airplane tickets or hotel rooms.

But they still have to beat the rake, and the rake is not inconsiderable. And so we are engaged in the question of how to maximize our potential profit. Beyond grinding out a decent hourly win rate, how can you *control* and *dominate* the online game, and set yourself up for major, significant wins?

One thing you can do is just *bet it up*. Find a table of Cally Wallies, players happy to limp in often and raise rarely. Then start raising all the time. If they're comfortable playing for one betting unit, make them play for two. If they're happy with two, make them go four. Online players can be taken outside their comfort zone, just as players in a real-world game can thus be made to sweat. By arbitrarily doubling the stakes of the game, you put yourself in position to run the table.

There's a downside to this, one you won't find in the real-world game: Since it's so easy to leave the online game, when you start going ballistic bully in the game, you'll have trouble keeping your customers. Smart and scared players alike will not want to hang around with the likes of you. In the b&m, they may be stuck with you because there are no other games available. Online, they can be gone in the click of a mouse. While there's a certain amount of ego gratification involved in seeing them run for cover, it certainly doesn't help your bottom line.

In the real world, you could use jokes and conversation, protestations of luck, and other image plays to keep your fish on the hook. You could train them to be happy to lose to you because you're such a nice, happy-go-lucky guy. How can your online foes know what a nice guy you are? How can they be trained to stick around and lose? Is it possible to use image plays online to disguise your ballistic bully tactics?

Yes . . . to a certain extent. I've already related how bullies use online chat to push other players around or put other players on tilt. I would now suggest that you use online chat to the exact opposite effect: not to push your enemies around, but to put them off their guard.

Most players don't chat during play. Maybe they don't know how to type, or maybe they don't want to lose focus. Perhaps they don't want to be seen as a *chat dork,* someone who engages in meaningless, pointless chatter just to pass the time. You may not be inclined to chat either. You may consider your chat to be so transparent an image play as to be utterly worthless. Yes, it's transparent, but no, it's not worthless.

Chat a lot. Chat disarmingly. Ask questions about where your foes are from: What's the weather like? What time is it there? (As a secondary benefit, they might actually tell you the truth, so that you'll discover who's playing poker in the wee small hours of their morning.) When you win, talk about how lucky you are. When you lose, talk about how talented *they* are. Maybe no one will believe a single word you say. So what? It's immaterial whether they view you as a liar or a fool. In either case, their view is influenced by *what you have to say.* In both cases, they're less likely to see you as you really are: a highly dangerous player using a disarming line of chat to keep everyone coming back for more.

Why don't they just turn off their chat function? Some will—so what? Most won't, because your chat is not offensive, just silly. They won't feel overtly threatened by it. Do it right and they'll actually enjoy hearing from you. They'll feel like you're livening up the game. Good for them; they're getting a show. Good for you; you're *running* the show.

You raise into a full field of callers in late position with pocket tens. You know you'll probably have to hit a set to win, but you know also that you're getting odds to try. Sure enough, you catch lucky (the one time in eight you will), drive the betting all the way, and extract maximum profit from the situation. If you remain mum here, the other players may tire of tangling with a bully like you. But throw a little chat out there

Boy, did I get out ahead of my hand there. Whew!

and you'll have at least some of them believing that you *did* catch lucky, and probably won't be so lucky next time.

Does this stuff work? Yes, it works, on the weak-minded or naive player—*exactly* the sort of player you want to engage. Though sophisticated foes might see through you, what's the worst that can happen? If they chat back at you, you win, because now they're thinking about you and not about them. If they get fed up and leave, you win, because who wants sophisticated foes in the game anyway?

I'm always happy to see my antics drive good players from the game. You should be too.

Once, just for the hell of it, I started typing in random strings of letters and sending them out as chat.

Klhe he;kl zie shex heieie89e

At first people thought there was something wrong with my software. Then they thought there was something wrong with my brain. Then they admonished me *"English only, please,"* and even had a site host drop by to remind me of that rule.

So I switched tactics.

I wrote English only, but nonsense English.

Proud face Lester foggy bottle kale.

Huh?

symptom System orange

Man, speak English!

But of course I *am* speaking English, so what can they do except shut off their chat function, filter out my chat specifically, or deal with it and move on?

There is *very little* margin in this kind of antic, but not *no* margin. If I establish myself as either a lunatic or an anarchist, again, those are two images at variance with the real facts of my play. In fact, since I'm playing selectively aggressively, and folding more hands than my foes, I probably have more time to fine-tune my text for maximum effect. I'm also not being bored, and that's huge.

Ballistic bully (with happy chat) is a two-pronged attack on your foes. First, you use the power of the raise to push them out of their comfort zone. Then you use happy chat to beguile their minds. Either strategy will work well on its own—bully betting will give you control of the game and wild chat will sow seeds of confusion—but taken together they become an iron fist in a velvet glove, yielding extra profit for you.

PROFIT FROM REGULARS

As you troll the sites for profitable playing opportunities, you're bound to run into some of the same players over and over again. Sometimes it seems as if you see them *every* time you log on, to the point where you find yourself thinking, *Man, does this guy not have a life?* (Of course, what does that say about you?) Then again there are other regulars whom we might call semi-regulars. You see them often enough to have book on them, but not so often that they're constantly underfoot. Just as you would in the real-world game, you want to have a dedicated strategy for dealing with your regular foes.

First, try to see yourself from their point of view, and imagine what kind of player they rate you to be. Do they see you as aggressive? Clueless? Out of control? Once you've got a picture of their picture of you, you can start to use this information against them. If they imagine you're loose, play tight; you'll make money on their calls of what they perceive to be your loose bets. If they think you're a bully, go right on being a bully, for if they show no willingness to battle back, they're giving you a free ride to their money. If they have no picture of you whatsoever, try to create one in their minds, by calling attention to your image with your chat.

> Hey Bosco, did you see the draws I was making last night?
> Never played so stupid in my life.

Your stronger foes won't fall for this, but as we've already determined, you've no business being at the table with those foes. That's why you have book on your regulars.

Next, review your book and remind yourself what works against these players. Do they fold in the face of scare cards? Bluff into them when the board shows flush or straight. Do they raise only with premium hands? Then get out of their way. You need never go to war armed only with hope when you have knowledge to rely upon instead.

Most players don't imagine that their play is so predictable. They certainly don't imagine that you're paying enough attention to them for these trends to appear and become useful. Why? Remember that, that just as they're nothing more than a screen name to you, that's all that you are to them. Just as you tend to underestimate the strength of unseen foes, so do they. Above all, *each of us is the center of our own universe.* It takes an act of will to imagine that other universes even exist. No matter how diligently your foe keeps book on you (highly unlikely, if you've chosen your foes correctly) he will have difficulty conceiving that you keep book on him.

Several times in the past, you've seen him bet into a board like, say, J-T-5. You've put him on top pair or middle pair, and many times you have folded in the face of his raise. But now your book reveals the following consistent pattern of his play: if an ace or a king hit on the turn, he has a strong tendency to check-fold, crediting any betting opponent for having hit a premium overcard. He may have been correct to do so, *but he wasn't correct in letting you find out!* Now if you find yourself in a borderline call/fold situation against him, you can lean toward calling, knowing that you can consider any ace or king to be an additional out for you.

This sort of overcard bluff on the turn is not all that uncommon, of course; good real-world players make this play every day. But they don't often make it knowing for sure that it will achieve the desired result. A percentage play, it only has to work a fixed fraction of the time to be profitable. Your book on your foes, however, can skew this percentage way in your favor, to the point where you know that certain plays in certain circumstances are virtual locks. These are the circumstances you seek to discover and create, of course, and two factors aid your endeavors: your strong and detailed book, and your foes' tendencies to fall into patterns.

Your path to victory against regular opponents, then, reduces itself to a fairly simple recipe.

1. Make book on frequent foes.
2. Study your records for plays they routinely make.
3. Devise strategies to exploit those routines.
4. *Attack!*

Suppose you've taken up seven-card stud high-low split, eight or better for low—called seven/8 for simplicity. In that game you'll find many players who do these two things with almost dead certainty:

- They play any starting hand containing three low cards.
- They fold if they brick out on fourth street.

If you can develop reliable book on these guys, they might as well just hand you their wallets, because you can play any starting hand whatsoever, figuring to scam the pot when they fail to hit a fourth unmatched low card, which will be more than two-thirds of the time. Yikes! What an opportunity! And it's yours for the taking, just because you pay attention to trends.

To review, there are two things to do with your regular foes. If they're truly strong, unpredictable players, don't mess with them. Only your ego will be served by the joust, and your bankroll could be severely pummeled in exchange. If they're not strong and they are predictable, build your database to the point where your predictions are reliable, and then go after them. They'll be there to give you their money until they learn to wise up and stay away.

CANDY FROM STRANGERS

Mostly you won't face regulars, of course. The universe of players is so large that the mere law of averages dictates that most of your foes will be unfamiliar. It would be a shame to let them keep their money just because you haven't had a chance to build book on them. What to do?

First, chat them up. Find out, if you can, whether they're new to poker, new to the site, or just new to you. They may not tell you the truth, but they probably will, for most (weak) players want online poker to be at least partly a social experience and in any case they don't yet know what a devious, dangerous foe you are, and haven't yet learned not to buy into your mental gymkhana.

Second, watch them closely. Within a lap or two around the table, you should be able to garner some useful information about the way they play. Don't worry too much about consistency at this point, and don't put too much stock in your conclusions. Just because you see Sunny1 raise one time on the button, for example, that doesn't necessarily mean she's a fan of the real estate raise; she may actually have a hand this time. On the other hand, if she throws away her blind even once, then you can eliminate her from the category of players who *always* defend their blinds. You're building book already.

Third, feel them out. Make some raises early on, just to see how a foe reacts. Does he raise back? Is that a peeved reraise, or did he really have a hand. This kind of discovery raise, also known as active sonar, is a good way to find out the relative fortitude of a new foe. One thing you always want to know about another player is: Will he play back at you? You won't know this unless you play into him, so go ahead and try pushing him around. He might just fall over completely.

At this point I'm back to talking about basic Killer Poker. Especially against new foes, it never hurts to be regarded as the big force at the table. They don't know you; let them learn to fear you. Not to underestimate your foes, but I think it's safe to treat the unknown enemy as weak until proven strong. If your new foe is crafty and tricky, it won't take you long to find out. The first time she check-calls the flop and check-raises the turn, you can tell yourself, "Well, she's capable of that." Then you adjust. You simply avoid direct confrontations with her until her true colors are shown. Did she make that move because her cards commanded or because she was putting a little active sonar back on you?

At the same time it doesn't hurt to let your enemies underestimate you. Suppose you're new to a table and find that a certain player seems to be attacking you a lot. In the early stages, when you don't yet have a reliable line on him, there's absolutely no harm in letting him think he can push you around. Establish yourself as timid and weak, and he'll give you no credit whatsoever when you suddenly turn tiger later. The first law of Internet poker—information is power—suggests that you save your aggressiveness for times when the balance of information has tilted in your favor.

I seem to be offering contradictory strategies, I know. On one hand I'm suggesting challenging your foes right away to test their mettle. On the other hand, I advocate laying back and waiting until you know your foes quite well. Can I wriggle off this particular hook with the claim that these strategies are not contradictory but rather complementary? Against foes who appear passive, be aggressive. Against foes who appear aggressive, be passive. With the passive ones, you'll win right away. With the aggressive ones, you'll gather the data you need to win later.

QUICK TAKES

Here are some brief looks at strategies and tactics for online play. Some of these are not unique to the online game, but their utility is altered by the Internet environment.

Ban on Advertising

In most cases, the composition of an online poker table changes so quickly that there's really no point in making any so-called advertising plays. In the real-world, where you could figure on four or five hours of staring at the same faces, you might try a stunt like raising under the gun with 6♥ 7♥, hoping to catch a hand you can show down, and thus advertise yourself to the table as a clueless lunatic. Make that play online and you're just throwing away your bets, because most of the players won't be around long enough for you to get a decent return on your advertising dollar.

A further argument against advertising is that it shouldn't be necessary. If you're challenging weak players, not strong ones, then you ought to be able to win with a straightforward push of premium hands. And if you're not in that circumstance, *goodness, why not?* The game you're in should be a *terrific* game, where advertising is useless because no one's paying that sort of attention. If the game you're in is *not* terrific, go find one that is.

Hit and Run

Players in the real world often feel uncomfortable about sitting down at a table, winning a few hands quickly, and then clearing out. They feel that they're violating some kind of weird poker etiquette that says that if you win their money in a hurry you have an obligation to stick around and give them a chance to win it back. Or maybe they don't like the feeling of the other players staring daggers in their backs as they walk away. Manifestly this is not a problem online, where your absence could as easily be explained by a disconnect or a dinner bell as by your own avaricious desire to take the money and run.

Some games are only good for a short period of time and should be treated as hit-and-run opportunities. It typically happens, for instance, that you join an extremely shorthanded game and find yourself alone with one or two easily dominated opponents. So long as you have them to yourself, you can strip-mine their bankrolls—but you won't have them to yourself for long. In a matter of moments, your shorthanded nirvana might turn into a full-table grind. Don't hesitate—*scoot!* There's another hit-and-run opportunity waiting for you back in the lobby or at another site.

The successful online player is light on his feet and deft and swift about changing games. He knows that there's *no reason* to remain in any game that's less than primo, whether he's been there for five minutes or five hours so far. If you're new to online poker, you'll have a little trouble adjusting to the hit-and-run methodology, but practice it a little and you'll see what a valuable tool it can be.

To use this tool effectively, you have to be prepared to hit-and-run even in the face of negative outcomes. It's no good attempting to peel off some bets from one or two opponents only to find yourself on the wrong end of a hundred-unit swing. If you're running bad—*run!* Don't worry that you didn't "book a win" in this session. Remember: your poker career taken as a whole is one long session and individual outcomes just don't matter. To quote the sage, "You're born broke, you die broke, and everything else is just fluctuation."

Seat Change

In the b&ms, changing seats can be one of your most frustrating undertakings. You have to inform the dealer that you want a seat change, then wait for another player to leave the game, then make your move, then wait for the blinds (or post out of turn), then get back in stride and play on. If you've made the move for strategic reasons (to get downstream from a strong player, for example), you may need to disguise that fact with noise about moving for a better view of the TV set or for luck or whatever.

Changing seats online is a much easier proposition. Leave the table, rejoin the table, take your new seat, post or wait, play on. No need to explain your actions to anyone. Maybe they assume you've changed to gain position, but they can't question you to your face, so let them live with their assumptions. It's so easy to change seats online that there's never any reason to sacrifice position to anyone—though one could argue that if position is an issue against a certain foe, you may be better off leaving the game altogether, for there's also never any reason to stay in a game where anyone has the better of you.

In any event, get used to changing seats, as you're used to changing games. Changing seats online is much easier and much quicker than in the real world; it's an opportunity that should not be overlooked.

Exploiting Double-Dippers

If you're working the lobby effectively, you'll know when you're playing against someone who's playing in two games at once. When you detect a double-dipper, you should be much more willing to mix it up with him, for a couple of reasons.

First, his attention is divided between the two games. It's not likely that he's giving either game the benefit of his best focus. Second, action in the other game can influence decisions he makes here. Watch him playing that other game. If you find him involved in a big pot over there, go ahead and attack his blind over here. He'll be more likely to surrender the one bet here and give the other game his momentary full consideration.

Does this seem like a small edge? Well, it is. Rare is the time that you'll find yourself able to exploit this particular situation. But there may be other situations you can exploit at the same time. Elsewhere at this table are players on whom you have strong book, plus a couple of Cally Wallies. Add them together with the double-dipper, and suddenly you're dominating half the field or more. Success online comes from the accumulation of small edges.

To Show or Not to Show (Your Cards)

The online game gives you the electronic choice of showing or mucking your losing hands, and showing or mucking your winners when everyone else folds. In general I prefer not to show any card I don't have to show—why give away information for free? However, there may be times when, for strategic reasons, you want them to know what you played. If you're up against someone who calls too much and she happens to fold and you happen to be able to show her absolute cheese, you can train her to call that much more.

But some players show cards because they want to show you what good draws they had (so you can commiserate) or simply because they don't know enough to click the "muck losers" button. Don't *ever* be a person who shows cards without good cause. If you haven't mastered the software, you shouldn't be playing for real money. If you haven't mastered your ability to swallow a bad beat, you're likewise in the wrong game.

Show cards for reasons of deception or to reinforce others' mistakes. Don't show for ego or just because you don't know enough not to.

Oh, and if they ask you what you had, lie.

Stay in Line

A point that bears repeating: Internet poker has a way of loosening everyone up. It's very hard for anyone to maintain their playing discipline over time, especially in the area of hand selection. The cards aren't cards but just pictures on a screen. The disrespect of other players is an abstract concept. Even the money seems completely unreal. These factors combine to create an environment where loose calls are the norm—and in an environment where loose calls are the norm, you want to make them too.

Guard against this. Remind yourself of basic truths like *little cards are poison in hold'em* and *no ace is no hand in seven/8.* If you find yourself playing weak cheese, just because everyone else is, excuse yourself from the game and go do something that won't cost you so much money. Don't let go of your starting requirements. If you do nothing other than play quality cards and quality cards alone, the online environment can be a profitable place for you.

But if you surrender your discipline, you'll soon surrender your bankroll too.

Discipline. Focus. Control. Don't play bad hands. It's really as simple as that.

Play More Tournaments

Online tournaments, especially the one-table shootout variety, offer a couple of very favorable opportunities. They give you good value for your dollar, ensuring a lot of play for very little money. They also provide an arena where book is of less overall importance. In a one-table shootout you're only going up against nine opponents, and that's nine opponents whose relative intelligence, trickiness, and aggressiveness you can easily discover in time for that information to be useful. Of course it's even better if you have book on some or many of them, but even if they're all unknown, this is a "one-off" opportunity for the Killer Poker player to strike.

Beyond the immediate advantage of being a money-making proposition, online tournaments offer tournament experience with real-world benefit. While the online tournament is not exactly like a real-world tournament, it's more like a real-world tournament than online ring play is like real-world ring play. Tournaments are all about analysis and deduction, and you'll find yourself using—and honing—skills in online tournaments that actually do carry over into real-world tournament situations.

Online tournaments are so cheap, immediate, and plentiful, they really afford you the opportunity to immerse yourself in tournament play and raise the level of your tournament expertise, on your time and your terms, at a very reasonable cost.

As a final benefit, tournaments have definite ends. If you don't know when to quit online, just sign up for a tournament and play till it's over or until you bust out. Let the end of the tournament be your exit strategy, and you'll keep OMHS at bay.

OVERALL STRATEGY FOR SUCCESS

In *Killer Poker: Strategy and Tactics for Winning Poker Play,* I proposed the following strategic stance: "Go big or go home." Players who win lots of money in any poker milieu are those who do what it takes to dominate the game. They're not afraid to raise and they're not about to be pushed around. They're bullies, and they like being bullies. Thus, they prosper.

This is doubly true online because the pace of play is doubly fast. If you can pit yourself against opponents whom you can push around and put to tricky decisions, you'll make extra money because they'll make extra mistakes. When you go online to play poker, you should always be in *full challenge mode.* The minute you're just there to relax and have fun, you're wasting your time, and your profit opportunity.

So before you jump into any online session, take a moment to psyche yourself up. Remind yourself that it's better to raise than to call, and dedicate yourself to making everyone else at the table *aware* of you and *afraid* of you. Be the boss. Take control. Go big or go home.

Herewith, then, the ten commandments of online poker:

1. There's bound to be a great game somewhere.
2. Your book is your best friend.

3. Information is power.
4. Play tournaments for practice and profit.
5. Solid, straightforward, and strong takes the money down.
6. Success comes from the accumulation of small edges.
7. Find the fish!
8. Make the most of your mobility.
9. There's no reason, *ever*, to let a stronger foe mess with you because . . .
10. There's bound to be a great game somewhere.

Anyway those are my ten. Now what are yours?

1. _____

2. _____

3. _____

4. _____

5. _____

6. _____

7. _____

8. _____

9. _____

10. _____

10

PHENOMENA OF ONLINE PLAY

This chapter takes a look at a few more special circumstances that arise only in the online environment or take on special significance there. They're offered here as further evidence that the Internet game should in no way be seen just as an electronic version of a live game. They're two different things, and success in one doesn't necessarily guarantee success in the other.

IT'S A FISH-EAT-FISH WORLD

It has long been known that, because of positional advantage, money in a poker game flows clockwise around the table. In all poker games, though, there's a larger flow, the inexorable flow of money from bad players to good players. From time to time, luck reverses this tide, but in the long run, the best players will win the most money.

In a closed poker environment, such as a small-town b&m, this can have the effect of consolidating money in the hands of a few good players. Absent the influx of new money or new players, eventually Big Al Kayda and Smooth

Jack Lowe will hold all the chips, and the game will come to an end.

The online environment, which is neither wholly closed nor wholly open, seems to have evolved a different version of this phenomenon. Money flows from weak players to strong players, but it makes a few stops along the way.

Poker online starts out with a vast pool of money held by all players across a fairly narrow band of limits. Within this playing population there are abundant very bad players, a few reasonably good ones, and a small minority of great ones. Since the great players are small in number, their impact on the overall distribution of money is not great—there simply aren't enough of them to make a difference. They don't mind, though, because the reasonably good players are out there doing their work for them.

Bad players lose to everyone. After they get done losing to each other, most of their money ends up in the hands of the reasonably good players, because the reasonably good players comprise the largest net-plus playing population in the game. Now, with more money consolidated in fewer hands, the net-plus players comprise a population of players who are good, but yet inferior to the best players. They're big fish, having won all that money from the little fish, which they'll now turn around and give to the top fish.

It happens every day.

BlueMoon is a fairly skilled, mid-limit hold'em player. He doesn't bother much with book, but he does keep a list of absolute weakies that he likes to track down and pummel. On this particular day, he has had great success in this endeavor and has pumped up his initial stake of $500 to more than $2,000. Now he goes looking for new targets of opportunity, bumps up a limit or two, and jumps into a shorthanded game against Clarify and AngieO'Plasty. Clarify isn't much of a player, but Angie is an absolute demon, dedicated to her online play and compulsive and comprehensive with her book. BlueMoon has never played against her before—but she has watched him play and identified a couple of reliable flaws in his game.

(A point worth stressing here: Angie has watched Blue-Moon play. In the name of doing her homework, Angie, like the best online players, spends a good chunk of her online play time *not playing at all*. She wants to have the advantage of knowing her foes even before they meet, and she knows that this advantage is available to anyone willing to just sit and watch for any decent length of time. The combination of railbirding and building book makes this experience intellectually fulfilling for Angie; she's never bored, and she's already making money.)

Now BlueMoon and Angie mix it up. At first, BlueMoon thinks he has the best of this situation, because his foe seems awfully passive, remarkably willing to surrender her blinds. He doesn't realize that Angie has detected Blue-Moon's tendency to push hard at any uncontested pot, so she's just waiting for a chance to trap him for many bets. Once she achieves this goal, she immediately turns on the heat, going from passive to super-aggressive in an instant. Suddenly BlueMoon is back on his heels. Angie isn't at all the player he thought she was. Now he calls a bluff that isn't, runs a bluff that doesn't, and finds his $2,000 reduced to $1,000 in a scant fraction of the time it took to win it.

In the real world, he'd never have found himself in this situation. In the real world, he *never* plays shorthanded, and he never sticks around when he sees he can be beaten. But here in the privacy of his own home, staring at a joke name on the screen, he can't believe this foe has his number. He thinks he's just running bad. He won't run scared, so he'll eventually run all the way down to zero. Tomorrow we'll find him back among the monkeyfish, trying to build his bankroll back.

Tomorrow we'll find Angie lying in wait for another bankroll to bring itself to her.

So there you have it: the big fish eat the little fish and the biggest fish eat them in turn. Occasionally the fish migrate from site to site, but the essential ecology remains the same. Many very bad players consolidate money in the hands of a few good players, who turn around and pass it over to the best. What lessons can we draw from this?

The first lesson is obvious: Be the top fish. Be the strongest, biggest, nastiest perch in the pool and take *everyone*'s money. That's a nice goal, but it will only happen if you're willing to wed top poker skills to an almost fetishistic devotion to online play. Short of this total commitment, you can't hope to be top fish.

Which leads us to the second lesson: Avoid top fish. If you find yourself accumulating a good-size bankroll, guard it jealously. Remember how you got it—by beating up on weaker players—and keep doing that. Attack known targets of opportunity. Stay away from unknown players with large stacks. There's no guarantee that their large stack means that they're great players; they might just be lucky or well heeled. But why take a chance? There are so many fish in the sea that you don't have to mess with the ones who even *look* scary.

You can, of course, gauge their skill by railbirding their play. You can watch the big stacks in action and discover whether they're big talent or big luck or just big buy-in. You'll find the latter the least likely to be true. Most people are so leery of putting big money into Internet poker that they tend not to buy in for huge amounts. If you see someone with a lot of chips, chances are he got there by winning.

Nor can you necessarily let down your guard if they

don't have a big stack, for they may have left most of their money in their player's bank. The only reliable way to know the quality of a potential top fish is to *watch him play.* Don't commit your money against him until you know for sure that he can't dominate you. In a world where the top fish eat the big fish and the big fish eat the little fish, it's only a silly or a lazy fish who allows himself to get eaten at all.

IRREALITY

The poet Wallace Stevens said, "Reality is things as they are." Reality in b&m poker is live players breathing in and out, pushing cards, chips, and money across a table. Reality in Internet poker is two to ten people separated by continents and time zones interacting with one another in a limited and highly stylized fashion through client software they all share. Internet poker as you experience it in your home, then, is a manifestation or interpretation of a poker game's reality, but not the reality itself.

To see this distinction more clearly, contemplate the difference between a nude and the picture of a nude. Each image may have the same psychological and physiological effect on you, but your interaction with the picture will be, well, abstract at best.

I'm not saying that b&m poker is to sex as Internet poker is to masturbation, but . . . okay, I am.

Internet poker, then, is not just unreal (not real), it's also irreal (not *capable* of being real). We understand this intuitively. No one has to tell us that Internet poker is a different kettle of fish. We also understand that while the game lacks b&m poker's physical reality, the money involved is equally real.

But yet, over time, the online money takes on a danger-ous irreality—dangerous because we lose our capacity to take it seriously. As I've already mentioned, moving money in and out of an online game is not so easy as moving money in and out of your pocket. Most Internet money, then, tends to stay on the Internet, and whereas real-world money can be used for many things, money parked at an Internet poker site can only be used for playing poker there. Eventually, if we're not careful, we forget that it has any other utility or value at all.

Eventually, if we're not extremely careful, we become extremely careless.

It's mentally easier to call an online bet because it's *physically* easier to call an online bet. You need only tap a finger on a mouse button. You don't have to lift the chips, push them forward, and place them in the pot; you don't have to say goodbye to your money in a tangible sense, which makes letting go of it a snap.

This isn't necessarily a problem all the time—but it doesn't have to be a problem *all* the time to do serious damage to your stack. A momentary lapse of concentra-tion, and those bets are gone, gone, gone, never to be seen again, absent hard work better spent on *winning* than on *winning back*. I'm reminded of the struggle to save giant redwoods: Protecting them is a matter of decades or cen-turies of vigilance, but it only takes a day to cut one down. If you intend to protect your redwoods (your stack), you must commit to eternal vigilance. The moment you make a "what the heck" bet or call, irreality has set in, and you must leave the game at once and not return until you can treat your online money with the sensible respect it de-serves.

Just as the irreality of your money can leave you vulnerable to careless calls, the irreality of your foes can leave you vulnerable to boneheaded plays. There are things we do online—ridiculous calls, raises, or bluffs—that we'd never, *ever* essay in the real-world game. Why? Because in the real world, we can see our foes, or more to the point, *they can see us.* We don't want to get caught in a boneheaded play in the real world because we don't want to *feel shame.*

We fear to have someone look us in the eye and call us foolish to our face.

Online, the barriers between ourselves and our real opponents tend to mitigate this fear. So what if we're completely out of line? So what if we're making a manifest mistake that's costing us a bunch of bets? At least it's not costing us *shame.*

You could argue—and I'd be right there by your side—that this consideration of shame has no place in poker. You could argue that a player who's thinking about saving face rather than saving bets is thinking about the totally and completely wrong thing. Well, guess what? People think about the wrong thing all the time in poker. We're glad they do, for we make money off their mistakes.

So long as we're not making the same mistakes.

It's an interesting thing, this aversion to shame. It can actually keep b&m players from playing worse than they do. If they don't make boneheaded plays for fear of experiencing shame, well, they end up doing the right thing for the wrong reason. Absent that fear in the Internet realm, all sorts of craziness can break out.

It is important—*vital*—that you don't contribute your share. As with detachment from the meaning of money, be alert to the creeping boneheadedness of your play. If you feel irreality creeping in, if you find yourself saying, "I know this call is wrong, but at least no one knows it's me," that's the time to sign off, because now it's you who's thinking about the totally and completely wrong thing, and your bankroll is at risk.

These cases—the irreality of Internet money and the psychological safety of bonehead plays online—are just two more instances of how the online game vectors away from the real-world version. Intelligent and aware players recognize that not all the differences in play are extrinsic; that is, having to do with things outside. The most important differences are intrinsic, having to do with how we approach the game. Cardroom reality and online reality are very different, and this reality we forget at our peril.

PROMISCUOUS PLAY

I live in Los Angeles. If I want to play real-world poker, I have to carve out an appropriate block of time from my schedule, including travel time, no less than half an hour each way under the best of traffic circumstances—and how often does LA experience the best of traffic circumstances? In support of my decision to play poker, I need to clear my schedule of other obligations, put on the proper clothing, eat a proper meal, make sure both the gas tank and my bankroll are full, and undertake the task of getting from point A to point B. All of this takes planning, organization . . . in sum, volition. The decision to play real-world poker is always premeditated. Inevitably, a span of time must pass between the moment of decision and the moment of actual play.

Maybe you don't live in Los Angeles. Maybe you live in Texas, where cardroom poker is illegal. If you want to play poker, you have to organize a trip to Nevada or Louisiana or Mississippi. The lag between decision and destination is even longer for you. You or I might even change our minds en route and decide that we really don't have the head for poker today, and really shouldn't play. This gap between decision and destination actually gives us the luxury of monitoring our choice and making sure it's a good one.

Online, as we know, the lag between decision and destination is a matter of seconds. I could be in the middle of writing this very chapter and suddenly feel the urge to see a few flops. Next thing I know, I'm not here on this page, I'm off at www.toodlebet.com, investing hope and greenbacks on the doubtful promise of 7-8 suited. The decision to play online poker, then, is a *much smaller*, and therefore much more easily arrived at, decision than its real-world counterpart. In the real world, you have to work to play poker. On the Internet you don't.

We've already described the negative effects of bringing an unprepared mind into an online poker game, but it's worth exploring all the half-baked rationalizations a player can use to launch an online session—and open the door to disaster.

Recess

It's easy to lump online poker play into the same category as solitaire or other computer games and to use it the same way: as a break. That's fine for solitaire or hearts, but dangerous with online poker. Solitaire is an event with a definite end: you'll either win the game, or lose the game, and return to the thing from which you needed a break. Not so with online poker. How many hands will you play? How long will your break last? And how will you feel if the cards go against you, and your break ends up costing you not just ten minutes but ten big bets?

Reward

Heavy computer users find themselves using their computers not just as tools of their various trades but also to reward themselves at the end of a long day or a long work session. When I'm on a writing jag, I tell myself that a stimulating game of *Bug Dust* or *A Farewell to Arms and Legs* awaits me at the end of each chapter. The thought of the coming reward makes my job easier to do. But if I reward myself with online poker I'm asking for trouble, because my goals will be all screwed up. I won't be there to play perfect poker but rather just to reward myself for something else I've done. It's not likely that I'll find my way into my poker resource state under circumstances like this.

Revenge

This motivation wouldn't have crossed my mind if not for a frustrating phone conversation I just had. I don't need to bore you with my problems; suffice it to say that I'm presently caught between a piece of bum technology and the manufacturer's unwillingness to make good. Hanging up the phone, I look around the room and ask myself, "Now what?" And a little voice inside my head says, "Hey, JV, why not jump online and play a little poker? Make the bastards *pay.*" You don't need to be a rocket scientist, or even the manufacturer of bum technology, to see the flaw in this logic. The one who pays won't be the manufacturer's representative or even my online enemies. Given that angry poker is never quality poker, online or anywhere, the one most likely to pay is me.

Diversion

A guy calls you on the phone. He's a yammerer, the kind of guy whose answering machine is set to *announce only,* but for one reason or another, you know you must listen patiently and make appropriate sounds at appropriate times. Wouldn't this task be easier if you had something else to do? Why not log on to www.killingtimewithflops.com and play a few hands while the loudmouth gets his rant out of his system? You might even turn that boring phone call into a productive poker session.

Or, you know, not.

Time Sink

Does your spouse take forever to get ready to go out somewhere? Does it drive said spouse nuts when you sit in the front hall impatiently tapping your shoe? Not to worry! Internet poker is there to swallow up those few stray minutes and put them to entertaining use. So stay at your computer until the tapping shoe is on the other foot! That could work—so long as you can lock your concentration onto the game in an instant, and not let any thoughts of your dawdly spouse intrude. If you can't . . . well, it's only money, right?

There are two classes of motivation that bring us into an online poker session: (1) the desire to win money, and (2) everything else. Looking deep inside yourself, try to list all the things that trigger your decisions to play online.

_____

_____

Look, I'm not saying you should never play poker online except when you have the time and inclination to do it right. Or, okay, I am. But realistically, we know that there are times when other reasons bring us into online play. There are times, frankly, when all we want is entertainment or recreation or diversion or distraction. These are not likely to be prime money-making opportunities, so we should probably play much lower than our regular limits. That way, the natural mental imperfections we bring to the game won't damage us too much.

To put it in simplest terms, if you must kill time, or rage, or boredom, try not to kill your bankroll too.

11

ONLINE TELLS

In the movie *Rounders,* Matt Damon's character, Mikey, picks off a tell on John Malkovitch's character, Teddy KGB, by noting that Teddy handles his Oreo cookies differently depending on whether he's bluffing or holding a hand. An Internet version of this moment would not make sense. What would Teddy do? Type-chat to Mike, "I'm licking the filling of my Oreo now"? How could that possibly be a tell?

Many players shy away from Internet poker because they believe that poker is *all about tells,* and without access to face, voice, body and behavior tells, the game is not the game and should not be played at all. I trust by now I've made it clear that there are other, different, edges to be had in the online game, but still you *can't* look your opponent in the eye, you *can't* listen for the sound of held breath, you *can't* note a certain shakiness of hand as he slides his chips into the pot or splits an Oreo in two.

Which is not to say that there's no such thing as an on-line tell. In fact they are abundant, but in order to make the most of them, you have to broaden your definition of the word *tell,* and also modify the way you hunt them down.

This chapter looks at some common Internet poker tells and discusses how to detect them, and then how to exploit them, avoid them, or fake them in turn.

THE SECOND PEEK

Here's a simple tell that translates directly from the b&m realm into the Internet game—but only on certain sites, such as www.truepoker.com. Most online sites deal the cards face up, so that each player's cards are visible to him throughout the entire hand. This is particularly handy for games like Omaha and Omaha/8, in which many players suddenly find themselves not penalized for not being able to remember all four of their cards at once. On www.true poker.com (and possibly by now other sites as well) the software functions differently. Cards are face down, and the player must click on them to see them. The avatar lifts them off the virtual felt for inspection, as if lifting cards off the table in a b&m game.

Cute.

But a tell.

Suppose you're playing Omaha/8 at this site, or another site with similar functionality, holding A-A-x-x, and the flop comes J-T-9 rainbow. You're about to bet, when you notice not one, but two or three of your downstream opponents going back to look at their cards again. What does this action tell you? It certainly doesn't suggest that they're on low draws, for everyone who called on the strength of their low already knows their hand is toast. No, what it tells you is that they think they have straights or straight draws, and they're going back to check. Their second peeks should warn you against betting, for anyone with a made hand is going to pound you back, and anyone with a draw is unlikely to lose enthusiasm for it now. Those careless second peeks can save you many bets.

Exploit This Tell

Try to build a correlation between the second peekers and the hands they ultimately show down. Do they take a second look at their straight or flush draws, or do they return for an admiring glance at their powerhouses? At minimum, note which players *can't remember what they have.* The inability to recall two cards in hold'em, or even four cards in Omaha, indicates that this player lacks discipline, concentration, or memory—any one of which flaws can be fruitfully attacked by you.

Avoid This Tell

Look once. Just as you would in a b&m game, take a careful look at your hand, commit its contents to memory, then set it down on the table and never look at it again. If you find yourself absolutely unable to do this, restrict your online play to those sites where your cards are displayed to you throughout the entire hand.

Fake This Tell

Randomize your approach to looking at your cards. Sometimes glance once. Sometimes glance repeatedly. You could even click that mouse button seven or eight times between the flop and the bet. Your opponents won't know why you're doing such a frivolous thing—but *you* will know that you're doing such a frivolous thing just to train your opponents to expect frivolity from you.

In today's Internet poker environment, the second-peek tell has limited utility, simply because so few sites deal their cards in this "click to peek" fashion. Then again, as the software becomes more sophisticated, and the sites strive to emulate real-world experience more and more closely, we can expect the use of "click to peek," and the value of this tell, to grow.

Quiz

You're playing seven-card stud on a site with "click to peek" functionality. On Seventh Street, your opponent shows four to a straight and you have a pair in the air. She bets. While waiting for you to act, she peeks at her hole cards again. What do you make of this?

_____

_____

Unless you have reason to believe otherwise (a prior record of trickiness) take this tell at face value. Just as in the b&m world, a player on a bluff will tend to do little to call attention to herself, for fear that any untoward action on her part will cause you to call. It's more likely that our friend is proud of her straight and wants to admire it some more.

THE STALL

"Time!" cries a real-world player facing a river bet in seven-card stud. His board shows a pair of eights and his opponent has four to a flush. After fifteen agonizing seconds, our hero drawls, "Well, I might as well raise." Anyone watching this action would immediately recognize his stall as a false tell. He clearly has a hand that can beat a flush, but hesitates before raising in hopes of inducing a call. Does this transparent trick work? Sometimes.

Online, the time it takes a player to bet may or may not be a reliable indicator of his confidence or certainty. That is, some players genuinely have tough decisions to make and take their time in making them. Others just routinely wait for the clock to wind down, for the sake of the deception that's in it. Whether your opponent's delays are a real tell or a false tell is something you'll just have to learn to recognize over time. But let's look at the mechanics of the thing and see if we can't eke out a little edge in this department too.

Most sites, as you know, put a clock on each player's actions. Twenty to thirty seconds is typical, and if you take longer than that to act, you'll be timed out, and your hand will be folded. Players who don't know any better will act in very consistent and predictable ways. If they're confident of their holding, they'll bet, call, or raise right away. If they're not so sure, they may think about it for a moment before coming to a conclusion. Players who *do* know better don't want to give away any information of this sort to their savvy opponents, so they develop the habit of taking the same amount of time for all their actions, whether they're confident of their power, confidently bluffing, or whatever.

A complicating factor in all of this "I know that he knows that I know that he knows" double-think is that your foe may be stalling for reasons completely unrelated to the play of his hand. Perhaps his phone just rang, or he's changing a CD or a diaper. Maybe his Internet connection hit a hiccup. Maybe he spilled his drink. You just can't know, and since you can't know, this is one tell you want to try to correlate very strongly to past behavior. Ask yourself (ask your book), "Is this a player who's demonstrated time trickiness in the past?" The answer to this question should help you put an appropriate value to his stall at this time.

Exploit This Tell

If you feel that the tell is true, simply take it at face value and act accordingly. Suppose you're holding a good ace and you bet into a flop of A♥ 9♣ 5♣. Your single opponent hesitates before calling. Has he taken that time to calculate the odds for his flush draw? Or perhaps he's on the bubble about a call with an under pair. Either way, you can bet with impunity on any turn card except the remaining clubs, fives, or nines. If you don't trust the stall, then don't bet based on the stall; bet rather on your deeper understanding of this opponent and how he generally plays. In the best of all worlds, you have book on his proclivities *and* on the trustworthiness of his stalls.

Trust your instinct. Subtle as it is, over time, the difference between a real delay caused by a tough decision and a fake stall will become apparent to you on a gut level. A lot of times you can predict a delay based on the fact that you've put your opponent to a hard choice. The rest of the time, well, if the stall seems hinky, it probably is.

Avoid This Tell

Whether you intend it or not, the time you take to bet may very well give away something about the strength of your hand—or anyway something about how you gauge that strength. The best way to beat this tell is to take exactly the same amount of time for all online actions. A lot of experienced players use the *count five method:* They simply count to five before taking any betting action of any kind. Check, call, raise, or fold . . . they do it all on the count of five. In this way, they limit variables in the time it takes them to bet without significantly slowing down the game. Five seconds is plenty of time to make most common decisions in poker (considering also the time you have to think while waiting for other players to act), but of course if you feel you generally need more time, you can always use the *count seven method* or the *count ten method* instead.

Fake This Tell

Seek situations where the hand complements the tell. Suppose you're playing junk in an unraised blind against one opponent, and the flop comes 3-4-5. You both check. A 7 comes on the turn, a card that could easily frighten your opponent, who could easily figure you for a bare six with a blind hand. You wait . . . wait . . . wait . . . then bet, leading her to believe that your stall is a false stall to induce a call, when it's actually a *bluff* false stall to induce a fold. The fake works not so much because of the fake but because of the hand your opponent puts you on. That's why we use it when the hand itself will help us sell the misinformation.

There's one place in the online poker realm—tournaments—where the stall is used not as a false tell but in an attempt to shoot an angle. When a multi-table tournament gets down to two tables, and close to the money, it becomes in the interest of a short-stacked player to play as slowly as possible, in the hope or expectation that other short-stackers at other tables will bust out first, and he will move onto, or further up, the money ladder. You see this sort of stall in real-world tournaments, but attentive players, dealers, and tournament directors see to it that the abuse never gets out of hand.

There is a similar protection online. It's called a *time bank*. Not all sites protect their tournaments with time banks, but some do. They give each player a certain amount of time, above and beyond their natural per-hand allotment, so that if a player calls "time" in a tournament, either to make a tough decision or to fix a balky Internet connection, the time comes out of a pre-established reservoir of minutes. Use up the time in your time bank, and it's, "Sorry, Charlie, you fold." For honest players, the time bank provides a way of taking more time when they need it. For angle shooters, it puts a brake (albeit a not altogether perfect one) on their sleazy behavior.

Of course, online tournaments have tournament directors, too, so if you feel that someone is using stall tactics to unethical ends, by all means drop a dime. The offender will be hurried along, or folded out, or bounced, as the situation demands.

Quiz

You're playing $10–$20 hold'em against a selectively aggressive player who raises pre-flop. You hold pocket jacks out of position, so you just call, but then bet into a board of T-8-3 rainbow. Your foe raises and you call. A king hits on the turn. You check. After a *long* stall, your opponent bets. What should you do?

_____

_____

A selective-aggressive player is likely to have anything from two cards in the playing zone (ten through ace) all the way up to a premium pair. The fact of this, plus her studied stall, indicates that she's hit her king, but doesn't want you to wriggle off the hook. Perhaps she puts you on top pair, good kicker. She is now not afraid, but wants you to think she is. Absent good, strong book to the contrary, fold.

THE PRE-ACTION BUTTONS

As you know, most online sites let you choose to make certain decisions before the betting gets to you. The pre-action buttons let you set your intention to check, call, fold, or raise while players in front of you are still making up their minds. This is theoretically handy if you're multitasking and need those extra few seconds to grab a phone call or a hand in another game, but it really degrades the quality of your poker play by giving away a large and exploitable tell to your opponents.

Suppose you're in second-to-last position, sitting on a pair of eights and looking at a flop of A-K-T. With three opponents out against you, including one behind you, you figure that your dogballs are dogmeat, and so you click the check/fold pre-action button. This means you'll check if they check and fold if they bet. Now let's imagine that the person behind you likewise plans to check, but he's also paying attention to you. The bettors in front of you check and you check too. Because you're on pre-action, though, your check is *noticeably faster* than the other players'. The savvy opponent behind you can easily tell that you had pre-acted, from which he can judge that you're not happy with your hand and you're looking for a chance to muck.

Knowing that at least one of his three foes will fold if he bets, he concludes that a bluff bet here has at least a one-third better chance of succeeding. So he bets. The others fold and you fold too. By dint of free information, you have handed a hand away.

It's not only bad poker, it's also bad etiquette. Because the pre-action button makes your intent so clear, it has the same effect as if you had acted out of turn, penalizing the players who acted before you and giving advantage to those yet to act. Though ostensibly in place to speed up the action and make the game better for everyone, these buttons actually end up doing a selective disservice to your foes.

But let's say you're playing heads-up, so that the secondary effect on other players is not an issue. Pre-acting is still not a good idea, for it gives your foe a reliable line on your play. In heads-up hold'em, for example, both players will be taking a blind on each hand. If you get in the habit of pre-folding all your junk, pre-raising all your strong hands, and pausing to consider the relative merits of a middle holding, it won't take long for observant opponents to catch on. For the sake of saving a second or two, you're giving your enemies what amounts to a free look at your cards.

Just say no to pre-action buttons.

Exploit This Tell

If you detect that certain of your opponents are using the pre-action button (they are not hard to spot) use this information as I have in the previous example, letting it guide you off the fence when you face marginal decisions. Obviously if you find someone whose pre-action check indicates a tendency to fold in the face of any heat, by all means just go on the attack. Also, record players' use of pre-action buttons in your book, and cross-reference against other elements of their play. Do they only pre-act when they're weak? Do they only pre-act when they're strong? Do they check/call every draw? Even the knowledge that they *never* pre-act can be helpful, for those who never pre-act tend to be stronger, more experienced players than those who do.

Avoid This Tell

To never give away any pre-action tells, simply never use the pre-action buttons. If you're that impatient, or that eager to spend your precious seconds elsewhere, you probably should not even be playing in the first place. And if you think you're doing the table a favor by speeding up the pace of play, well, maybe you are, but why do that favor if it's going to leech money from your stack?

Fake This Tell

Assuming your foes are aware enough to notice, you can telegraph certain false intentions by judicious use of the pre-action buttons. You can, for example, attempt to induce a bluff by pre-checking a hand of significant power. If your foe interprets your swift check as a sign of weakness, he might just fall into your trap. Needless to say, if you suspect your opponent of faking this tell, you'll bet on the relative strength of your hand, and not what you imagine his intentions to be.

There is a certain amount of gamesmanship involved in the use of stalls, pre-action buttons, and other forms of online delay. These actions parallel real-world poker, where players will fake an intention to raise for the purpose of inducing a check or make strong actions with weak gestures and so on. Here again we see that while the online game doesn't offer nearly so rich a trove of direct face-to-face tell information as the b&ms, there *is* information to be had, and disinformation to be spread.

Quiz

Seat five has been swift-tight all night, folding most hands with the lightning-quick reflexes of someone making liberal use of the check/fold pre-action button. Now comes a hand where, after a delay of several seconds, he comes out raising. What should you do?

_____

_____

Two tells are at work here. The fact that he's come off his pre-action button indicates that he has a real hand. His stall suggests that he wants you to think he has a marginal raise. Since his use of the pre-action button has already tabbed him as a reliably tight player, you can conclude that his hand is real. Unless you have a premium hand yourself, you should fold.

CHAT TELLS

Norman Whitfield and Barrett Strong's classic song *I Heard It Through the Grapevine* offers the timeless advice to believe half of what we see and none of what we hear. When deciphering or decoding poker site chat, it's not so much a case of believing or disbelieving what you see or hear, but rather a matter of considering the source.

Sometimes, what they say is absolutely true, totally re-
flective of their feelings. Suppose someone takes a bad beat
from an inferior hand, and chats,

How could u play that cheese?

Chances are she's legitimately bent out of shape, and legitimately trying to ease her psychic pain by railing against
the moronic play of the dillweed who drew out on her. This
is chat you can take at face value.

Then again, perhaps a player makes a call on the end,
catching his opponent in a bluff. He may type something
intentionally disingenuous like,

Meant to fold. Hit rong button.

There's no reason to believe that this is anything but a
clumsy attempt to hide a deft call. Ignore this noise, or better yet, book it as evidence that the player behind it knows
enough to catch bluffs and also knows enough to try to disguise this fact—but not enough to do a credible job.

What about a situation where an ace hits the board on
the river, someone bets, everyone else folds, and the bettor
types this claim:

Caught my ace.

Is she telling the truth? Maybe. Maybe not. She could
make a case for claiming the ace whether she had it or not.
Maybe she wants you to think she bluffs. Maybe she wants
you to think the opposite. In this case, there's not enough
information to reach a trustworthy conclusion. So don't.
Take note of the chat, and look for other instances in the
future. A pattern will eventually emerge, for whether peo-

ple generally tell the truth or generally try to be deceptive, they *generally act consistently*. If our chatting pal thinks she's being cleverly devious this time, chances are she'll try the same strategy again later. Eventually you'll be able to correlate her chat with her actions and draw a bead on her real intention.

If nothing else, chat is a reliable indicator of mood. Someone engaged in angry or resentful or disparaging chat is clearly someone on the dark side of his mood, and should be exploited accordingly. Someone engaged in pleasant online persiflage is less likely to go on tilt out of rancor. Chat may also tell you an opponent's relative level of experience on a site. Someone who chats about the results of last night's tournament obviously spends at least some fair amount of time on the site and should be treated as an experienced opponent until the facts of his play suggest otherwise.

Exploit This Tell

In general, you exploit tell chats by simply taking note of who chats and what they say. Are they using chat to make the game a more "human" experience? Then they're recreational players and should be played into aggressively. Do they use chat to deceive? Without at all buying into their deception, you can reliably consider them deceptive in chat, and therefore probably deceptive in play. Do they bleed their emotion into their chat? *Attack!* Angry or resentful or frustrated players are a rich target of online opportunity because the only way they can fight back is by furious play, and furious play will undoubtedly veer away from perfect play.

Avoid This Tell

The simplest solution is never to chat, and this is the solution that most players use. They keep mum, play their cards, win their pots or take their beats, and move on. They genuinely don't care where you're from or what time it is where you live. If you draw out on them, they have no interest in railing against you or the gods. They'll just wait for a chance to take that money back. By simply *not chatting,* you can preserve and protect the perfect poker face that online play affords. Once you do start chatting though, be aware that you run the risk of giving something away to someone, whether you think you are or not.

Fake This Tell

If you plan to chat, I suggest *chat wild;* that is, tell the truth and lies by turn, feign innocence, represent experience, claim ignorance, spout nonsense, and basically just type and send any wacky thing that comes to your mind. This is the online equivalent of a crazy or "party" image in real-world play, with the advantage that you don't have to be an extrovert or a glib personality to pull it off. All you need is the willingness to type and send, and the willingness to be considered a fool or a nut or a brat. You should have that willingness for two reasons: One, it's the Internet; no one knows who you are. Two, whatever they think of you, if they're thinking about you at all you've gotten into their heads, and that's good.

Just as "they can't figure out your strategy if you don't have one," they can't get a line on your chat if the line you draw is never straight.

Considering the topic of chat tells in general, this is an

area you can comfortably ignore altogether if you're so inclined. The relative advantages and disadvantages of chat tells are marginal, especially when measured against the benefits of good, solid book and good, solid play. Some players find sending or receiving chat to be a distraction from the serious business at hand. If you find that you can't concentrate both on chat and on perfect poker, by all means disable your chat function and continue your session in silence.

Quiz

Playing $5–$10 hold'em, you fold and watch as just two competitors take a flop of A♥ 6♦ 3♥. After a bet and a call on the flop, the turn comes 5♦. Another bet gets another call and you see a river of 9♦. The same leader bets, but now the other player raises back, collects a crying call, and shows down J♦ T♦ for a 23-1 runner-runner flush. The losing player furiously types:

u NEVER had odds 4 that call!

Based on this information, how should you adjust your own play?

_____

_____

The chatter is right that her foe never had the correct odds to draw to her flush, which tells us that the caller has exploitable holes in his play. But the chatter has also let her temper show, which means that *she* has exploitable holes in her attitude. Attack both players! Don't let either one escape!

NICKNAME TELLS

We've already discussed the need to take care in selecting a nickname, so that you don't unintentionally give away information about your real-world whereabouts, skill level, playing style, or proclivities. Players who do not take such care—and their name is legion—are giving us a free peek inside their minds. It's a peek we ought not overlook.

Suppose you encounter a player whose nickname is RaiseEmUp! Would you expect that player to be clueless, weak, and passive? Naturally not. He may be clumsily deceptive, but if he were completely clueless, it wouldn't occur to him to be deceptive.

What do you make of the nickname Tex23? Can you conclude that this player is from Texas? Not necessarily. Maybe he's trying to project a cowboy image. On the other hand, a player who calls himself StockholmCharlie is probably honestly from Sweden, and taking guileless pride in his heritage. Good for him—national pride is wonderful. But now that you know what part of the world he's in, you know what time of day he plays his poker. Someone who goes at the game in the middle of the morning or the middle of the day is probably fresher and more clear headed than the proverbial midnight gambler.

Boys will be boys, they say—except on the Internet where boys may be girls, disguising themselves with feminine playing names or avatars. This is fairly solid deception in that there's really no way of knowing whether Daisy is a real girl Daisy or a boy Daisy masquerading as a girl Daisy or, for that matter, someone named after a dog Daisy. As with online chat and short-term statistical results, it doesn't pay to make too much of screen names unless you're certain that your read on the name is reliable.

Exploit This Tell

If a player calls himself NewKidInTown, you can't know for sure that he's new—so chat him up. Ask him about his nickname and see if he'll tell you how he arrived at it, and then decide whether you believe him. In the best case, his chat confirms his rookie status and you can do what we do to all beginners: Make 'im pay for lessons! You can also exploit this tell in a more general sense by using it to divide your foes into the classes of "tricky" and "straightforward." Though it's not a given that a tricky player will have a tricky nickname, someone who calls himself A-9ChrisF at least knows enough about poker to pay homage to the hand that Chris Ferguson held when he won the $10,000 buy-in no-limit hold'em championship at the 2000 World Series of Poker. An abject newbie would be less likely to take that name, just as an experienced pro would be unlikely to call himself SirCallsAlot.

To make the most of tells in a player's nickname, look for a strong correlation between the name they choose and the way they play. Make good, solid book on their play—then ignore their name altogether!

Avoid This Tell/Fake This Tell

As previously mentioned, put a certain amount of thought and care into selecting a nickname so that you don't inadvertently give anything away about your play. Suppose I used the online handle KillerPoker? It's appropriate enough, but an intelligent foe encountering that nickname is likely to conclude either that I'm a disciple of the Killer Poker style, or I'm an arrogant bastard who thinks he is. Either way, I present myself as someone who knows *something* about poker, and since that information is reliable, I don't want my enemies to have it. For safety's sake, choose a name that's opaque; one that reveals nothing about who you are, where you're from, or how much you know about poker.

Again, though, don't over-invest in this stuff. Just because a player calls herself YellowCab, you can't necessarily assume she's a cab driver. And even if you could assume that, would you then be safe in drawing conclusions about the quality of her game? Of course not. Take all screen names, even screen names like GrainOfSalt, with a grain of salt.

Quiz

Two one-on-one opportunities present themselves to you. Same game, same limits, but the player at table A is called MinisterOfSillyWalks and the player at table B is called BigPokerOktober. All other things being equal, which table should you choose?

_____

_____

Well, let's see . . . the Minister of Silly Walks was a Monty Python character, so that means that this guy is a Python fan: probably middle aged, possibly not all that serious-minded. BigPokerOktober, on the other hand, has named himself after an annual tournament at the Bicycle Casino, where he's possibly a regular. All other things being equal, then . . .

Choose *neither!* Names alone are not enough to go on. If you don't have book on either player, then ghost their play (against other opponents) until you do, or go find a foe whose (lack of) quality is already known to you. Don't let your own prejudices and hidden assumptions drag you into uncharted waters.

BEHAVIORAL TELLS

All sorts of online tells reveal not just how a player approaches a certain situation, but how he engages in the game as a whole. From these general behavioral tells, you can deduce the relative quality of your opponent's game and decide whether or not he's a good target for attack.

Double-Dipping

Playing two games at once is a *big, fat tell*. Your savvy opponents make a regular habit of checking out the action at all the tables on their online site. They can't help noticing that you're here in seat six and also in seat three over in the Omaha/8 game. What does this tell them about you? That you're cocky, confident, *and easily bored*. That you're more interested in entertainment than in winning. That you'll probably play inferior hands, because the same restless energy that puts you into two games at once will also put you into pots where you really don't belong.

Call Frequency

In monitoring which players fold, and how often, you're bound to discover some who rarely or never fold. What can you deduce about their play? That they're too loose, yes. But what can you deduce about their underlying state of mind? That they're either ignorant of proper poker play or that they *just don't care*. It's a given that some players, even real-money players (even big-money players), are only in the game for a good time. They call all the time because they just enjoy playing. Good for them. Let them call—and punish their calls with your quality hands. Above all, recognize that the *fact* of their play is a key to unlocking the *reason* for their play.

Short Money

A player who's underfunded in a game, any game, is giving away strong signals about her state of mind. Either she bought in short, a Scardy Scardeson afraid to put real stakes on the line, or else she bought in for a reasonable amount, which she has now lost, and is thus running bad. Attack short money, because the mere fact of a short stack means she's less likely to play strongly or well.

When you first join the game, take a look at those stacks. Find out who's loaded and who's not. If possible, you want to enter the game as the big stack and use the leverage of your chips to push others around. In any case, though, note where the short money is, because even though weak chip position can indicate a weakness of luck, it most often betrays a weakness of mind.

What other behavioral tells can you identify, and how can you exploit them?

_____

_____

Many people with no experience in online poker reject the game out of hand because they think the psychological element is absent. They are, in a word, wrong. That element isn't missing; it's just subtle. Where you might draw a lot of direct conclusions from the physical behavior of b&m players, the online equivalent requires more analysis and deduction—detective skills, if you will. This is why some real-world players don't prosper online: They're great at interpreting body language, but not so good with raw data or small pattern changes.

True, a certain class of tells is absent from the online game. But another whole class of tells, utterly absent in the real-world game, is available to the attentive online player. With that in mind, I would ask you, over the course of your online playing career, to keep a list of tells you discover. These tells will not only help you beat your opponents, the hunt for them will improve your ability to spot online tells and also raise awareness about any undetected tells you may have.

The tells are there. You just have to go find them.

12

♣ ♠ ♦ ♥

FOUND OBJECTS

"The ocean is blue and it's also wet." In other words, there's often more than one right answer. In this chapter, you'll find some very savvy "right answers" provided by some very savvy people. You'll also find some artifacts of the Internet poker phenomenon and some, if you will, relics of my research. I hope that all of this information, the wise and the whimsical alike, gives you new food for thought about your own approach to online poker.

§§§

Obviously the biggest difference between live play and online play would have to be the absence of physical tells. A great player's tell reading ability is neutralized online, which leaves just the fundamentals. If you have a good understanding of poker fundamentals, there should be no reason why playing online wouldn't be profitable. There are likely a few minor adjustments you would have to make when playing online though:

1. You will have to call potential bluffs more often. Without the presence of physical tells, the only way you'd be able to make a big laydown would be to have logged enough hours with your opponent and have a good read of his betting patterns. When playing online though, it's likely that you'll often face players you've never faced before. Against them, it's important to pay them off until you have enough information otherwise.

2. You should bluff less often. Again, if you are supposed to look people up more often than you normally would, then so should your opponents—and they will. So bluffing more than you need to is just a total waste of money. Your profit from these games comes from VALUE BETTING, not bluffing.

—Daniel Negreanu, 1998 WSOP pot limit
hold'em champion

§§§

qsm182: u can only win a certain amount in here then they
    shut ur cards down
qsm182: its bs
bigsandy: is thattrue?
qsm182: yup
Hanrahan: lol
bigsandy: i agree
Hanrahan: what's the cutoff, and how much have you lost
    so far?
qsm182: might as well be sitting in the corner . . . playing
    with urself
qsm182: 404 today
qsm182: no 40$
qsm182: not 1 hand
qsm182: its rediculous
qsm182: what surprises me is that i seem to be the only
    idiot in here that sees it
Elephant Man: see what

Hanrahan: you should read rec.gambling.poker. lots of people see it.

Elephant Man: SEE WHAT?????

Elephant Man: lol

qsm182: why isnt something being done about it?

Hanrahan: they have the limiter on him. he's won so much
at this site, he's not allowed to win any more

Elephant Man: ABOUT WHAT???

Elephant Man: WHAT???

qsm182: if u complain . . . they close ur account

Hanrahan: then why is yours still open?

qsm182: i havent said anything to them

qsm182: yet

Elephant Man: OK FINE DON'T TELL ME

qsm182: i did at paradise and was closed out

Hanrahan: i doubt that very seriously. you might have lost
your chat if you said the s.c.o.** word

qsm182: no . . . i complained about the cards and they
closed my account

qsm182: i should know

Hanrahan: how much did you lose there lifetime?

qsm182: 3000$

Hanrahan: i think i see the problem.

qsm182: f u

Hanrahan: you have to wear the foil shiny side out or it
doesn't work.

Elephant Man: After $150 I'd seen enuf of paradise

qsm182: no chit

CumGetSum: i hate paradise anyhow

CumGetSum: too many miracle cards win

Elephant Man: consensus is they're crooked

qsm182: they cheat

—verbatim chat excerpt (names changed)

§§§

If you can't stand the heat, go stand in the kitchen.

§§§

I keep extensive records on my opponents. This is specially ad-vantageous in my case because I play fixed limit and pot limit games (especially Omaha/8) online. I also play every type of tournament available online. My style varies and opponents dis-play different skills and weaknesses in response to my play. For example, I play in seven-card stud high-low tournaments against a player I'll refer to as "Spike" (not his screen name). Spike is adept at hand selection, strong at early street play, and decent at early phase tournament play, but he usually goes too far with a losing hand (farther than pot odds would prudently dictate). As the tournament progresses he fails to adapt to opponents' rela-tive chip positions (plays almost as if he's in a ring game). I also play in a $1/$2 blind Texas hold'em pot limit ring game with Spike. In this game, surprisingly, his hand selection is very poor (he fails to adjust for position). But, he plays the turn and river well (seizes opportunity nicely). I have recorded these tendencies (and more) on a Microsoft Word document. I keep one file per site . . . by screen name/alphabetically. It is a simple matter to maximize and minimize the document during play to ensure I have the right read on each opponent, a crucial part of poker. I keep extensive personal records. I list each site and my result by date and specific game (e.g., O/8 PL with $1/$2 blinds). I in-clude time of play for each session. When I play in Las Vegas I can be excused for failing to deploy optimum game selection. Many brick and mortar poker rooms spread only one hold'em game in the morning and I won't drive around town to find a *loose game. But when I play online, shame on me if I don't click around the popular sites to find a juicy game. It takes a few minutes, but several sites provide helpful information such as average number of pre-flop callers and average pot size for the last hour. Prudent game selection is an underrated aspect of poker in my opinion. The proliferation of online gaming and ease of site navigation facilitate game selection. Take advantage of technology to increase your win rate.*

—Lee Munzer, poker journalist

§§§

Don't treat the game like a game.

§§§

Most online players look for any excuse to play. They don't notice that you are a tight player. Just play your good starting hands and you will get plenty of action. Don't worry about disguising your play.

—Annie Duke, leading female money winner, WSOP

§§§

I would say if you can play perfect poker at the free-play tables, when there's no money at stake, you have a much better chance of prospering online, because this tells you that you're more concerned with process than with product. You want to play correctly—that's the most important thing.

—JV's online diary

The most important advice I can give players is to only play for money on legal sites. If an operator is willing to risk committing serious crimes, why would you expect him to run an honest game. How do you know if a site is legal? There are two easy criteria:

1) The site is licensed, hopefully by a reputable state or country; or 2) The site puts severe restrictions on who may play.

One of the great weaknesses of the Internet is that it has no editor. A site can claim that it is licensed, when it is not. So far, this does not appear to be much of a problem. Still, you should check with the various rating services to see if they list the site as being licensed. This also gives you a chance to look over former patrons' comments and complaints.

Normally, you would expect the larger jurisdictions to do a better job of policing their licensees than little states or island nations. This has not been true with Internet gambling. It is not that big countries are doing a poor job. Rather, smaller governments, like the Isle of Man, are trying to establish their credibility and appear to be doing just as good a job as the largest nation.

Even unlicensed sites may be legal. Poker is legal in some states. It also can be run as a game of skill, which would allow it to be played for money in other states. But the federal and state laws vary so much that legitimate operators would not take bets from everywhere in the world. If you see restrictions limiting players to a single state, you have greater confidence that the game is legal.

Of course, not every legal site will be run honestly. But would you rather bet at a licensed card club in California or a game run by the mob in the back room of a bar?

—I. Nelson Rose, author, *Gambling and the Law*

§§§

You wonder what online poker registration will be like ten years from now. (Retinal scan, automatic debit of $1,000 from a bank account associated with your mother's maiden name, and you're off and running!)

—Evan Viola

§§§

How many times must players get burned before they realize that online poker is not a place to play for serious money?

How many times must players place their trust in poker celebrity endorsements and get burned before they realize that online poker is not a place to play for serious money?

If it walks like a duck, looks like a duck, and quacks like a duck, it is a duck.

Dragon Poker, Highlands Poker, Pokerspot, etc. all were scams. They let players deposit money, operated long enough for the deposited money to become substantial, and then shut down. The owner/operators disappear, and the players' money disappears with them.

They were scams and the players who played there were suckers. The players at the currently running online poker sites are the suckers of the future.

It is time to admit that online poker sites in general are scams.

There is no regulation, no oversight, no governing legal authority, the firms are not audited and do not release ownership information or financial statements.

If you deposit any money in any of them, expect to be swindled in the future.

—"World Class Poker Player" from rec.gambling.poker

§§§

I would advise the online player to throw the "bluff" out of his repertoire for all limit games $5/$10 and below. Bluffs should be used on players who will lay down a hand and nearly all the small limit players will call you.

Another tip I would give is to treat the online game as you would a "real" game. By that I mean you should pay attention to the game. Many players check their mail or watch TV while playing online poker. It's easy to relax at home and write out bills or do other things while playing. A lot of players simply don't focus on the game and then wonder why their results may not be so good. Like in brick and mortar rooms, concentration is a key to success in online poker as well.

—Mike Sexton, poker champion; host, PartyPoker.com

§§§

*The purpose of winning is to have
enough money to play more.*

§§§

. . . And this is yet another argument for making sure that your bankroll is not just adequate for the limit you're playing at, but actually overadequate. Remember that your goal is to parlay your original stake into a self-sustaining bankroll, so that you

can play online as much as you want without having to throw more money at it. In order for this to work, you have to be able to withstand the swings that bad beats will throw your way. Play low. As low as you can stand to play. You're here for the long run, and you don't want short term fluctuation to send you scurrying back to FirePay for more dough.

—JV's online diary

§§§

>I'm looking for Internet poker sites, where I can play for real money against human opponents. I know one human opponent game (online casino at Compuserve). But this game isn't for real money, so the game is extremely loose and too easy to beat. Recs highly appreciated, Thx.

—rec.gambling.poker, 1997/10/04

Who the hell would want to play poker for money on the Internet anyway?

—reply, same day

§§§

I enjoy playing online poker when I do not have enough time to go to a brick and mortar cardroom. There are many benefits to being able to play at home such as not having to worry about dressing up to go out, not having to drive to the casino, not having to toke the dealer, etc. Of course I do miss the social aspects that are present in a b&m cardroom such as being able to see friends, meeting new people, and being able to observe "tells" in person.

Many people question whether or not the sites are honest. In my viewpoint, the sites operate 100 percent honestly as far as the

*actual randomness and card distribution is concerned. I do rec-
ommend playing on sites that have been in operation a long
time and that have big names behind them. Obviously players
could collude with each other via the telephone, instant message, etc. However I believe they will be caught over time. The
sites have great incentive to catch cheaters and many precau-
tions are taken to do so. They can go back and look at hand histories of suspected perpetrators and can easily confirm if
cheating has occurred.*

*I think online poker can be very rewarding. There are many new
players online, and the action at most sites is very good. Online
poker will help the number of poker players worldwide grow.*

—Linda Johnson, 1997 WSOP razz champion

§§§

*The point is that Paradise kidnaps almost all of your RAM and
won't give it back. If you're like me and get a little bored waiting
for the rest of the hand to play out, you might not like having
your RAM stolen from you. I've also found that waiting for a
table can be annoying. Sometimes a player will beat you to the
last open seat, or you'll get yourself situated at a nice comfy
table, only to discover that the table is breaking up, leaving you
staring at three other players and a computer-dealer saying
"Waiting for other players to join." I've waited as long as five
minutes at a table. Not long by Vegas standards, of course, but
practically an entire day sitting at a computer screen without
anything happening.*

—Evan Viola

§§§

*Online it's hard to tell an inspired read
from rank stupidity.*

§§§

*There's no place for whim online—any more than in a real
world game. It's just that whims seem like such a good idea
when no one sits in judgment.*

—JV's online diary

§§§

*I believe that Internet poker will be one of the greatest spurs to
the development of more players in the 21st century. People that
have no reasonable access to public cardrooms can now play for
small or large stakes in the comfort of their own home. It seems
only natural to conclude that the more players exposed to poker
the bigger it will become. Casino poker can only benefit from
this influx of new players. The people playing online will eventually want to try it in the casino environment. That includes
both tournaments and side games as well. There are always
some people that will try to take advantage of online poker by
collusion. That is in my opinion the biggest danger and threat to
the continued advancement of poker. There is nothing to stop
two people from playing in the same game and telling each other
over the phone what hands they hold. I know of no way to prevent this at the present time, except to be aware that the possibility exists and watch for unusual betting patterns from the
same two or more players. If something appears questionable,
report it immediately to the online site. The future of poker in*

my opinion is unlimited and will only get bigger and better, especially with more television coverage and corporate sponsorship. Online sites can only help in the long run, but they must be policed properly.

—Tom McEvoy, four-time WSOP champ

§§§

Number of Google hits for online poker*: 656,000*

§§§

What did we learn from this chapter?

- That people who chat online can't spell.
- That you can value bet Daniel Negreanu because he's not going anywhere on the river.
- That focused and attentive players win the money online.
- That the jury's still out on Internet poker's legality and integrity.

What else? *What else?* Write it down.

_____

_____

13

TIPS

Here are a few short grabs about the online game. You may find it useful to review these tips before each Internet poker session. Not only will this remind you "what's what" in online poker, it will also give you a period of smooth transition from "not playing" to "playing," thus bringing you to the virtual table better prepared for the battle to come.

COUNT HANDS

If getting away from the game is a problem for you, if you lack a good exit strategy, try this: assign yourself a session of, say 50 hands. Further assign yourself the task of tracking the outcome of all 50 hands, and then quit after the 50th hand. What you will find is that your focus stays much keener because you have a task to accomplish and also a very clear sense of when the task will end.

DON'T OVER-ASSIGN VALUE TO YOUR STATS

A stat board will tell you that an average of 33 percent of players are seeing the flop at one table and 50 percent at another table. In practical terms, that's a difference of one or two players per hand. That difference may be significant—but then again, it may not. It could be that one or two wallies have just left a given game, and that the see-the-flop percentages have not caught up with the change. A much more reliable indicator is to track players you *know* to be weak and loose, hunt them down and attack!

DON'T JUST JUMP IN

Take a few minutes to prepare your mind for online play. Remember that the normal time of transition that you get in driving to a club is absent from the online experience. For the sake of getting your head straight, take five or ten minutes to review your goals and strategies for the session to come. From the first bet forward, your decisions count; be prepared to make the right ones.

CHOOSE YOUR SCREEN NAME WITH CARE

Pick a name that doesn't give anything away about where you're from, how old or what gender you are, nor how you approach the game. If you do wish to give information of this type, make sure that it's misleading information. When you create your online persona, you get an opportunity to reinvent yourself completely. Make the most of that chance!

HAVE A SEPARATE CREDIT CARD FOR ONLINE TRANSACTIONS

Not only will this help you keep your poker bankroll separate from your other money, the fact that you're using the card only for Internet transactions creates a sort of firewall between these purchases and your other credit activity. If someone does steal access to this card, they'll be able to attack only your online credit, and not your credit house as a whole.

CASH OUT SOMETIME

If you find yourself ahead on an online site, don't forget to cash out some of your winnings and put them back in your pocket. Fail to do this and you run the risk of leaving your money in play until some unfortunate swing of negative fluctuation leaves you with nothing. Remember, profit isn't profit if you never get around to taking it.

DON'T BE A KID IN A CANDY STORE

When you first play poker online, you're bound to be awestruck and excited by the ease of the thing; in fact, by the mere *fact* of the thing. Being able to play poker for real money from home strikes many people with the force of revelation. Over time, the revelation will fade, and you'll be able to bring a good, stable, matter-of-fact attitude to the game. Until you settle in, try not to go berserk. It's only poker, after all.

WRITE NOTES TO YOURSELF

Alone at your Internet poker station, you can leave yourself written reminders about what to achieve and what to avoid. Write notes to yourself, and post these notes where you can see them while you play. A timely "If you can't raise, don't call" or "Have you passed the point of pain?" might put you in a profitable situation or keep you away from a perilous one.

GLEAN THE SCREEN

In online poker, your computer screen is a constant source of raw data about your foes, their trends and tendencies, the strength and weakness of their play. When you're not in the hand—at those times when your mind tends to wander—remember to glean the screen for this data. It's always there, and there's always something new to learn about someone. Gleaning the screen has the added benefit of keeping your attention where it belongs, fixed squarely on the game.

AT LEAST GLEAN *SOMETHING*

Even if you can't or won't commit to keeping major statistical information about your foes, do some basic, seat-of-the-pants stuff at minimum. If you do nothing more than parse your opponents out into the categories of *tricky* or *straightforward, strong* or *weak,* you'll go at least some of the way toward using the power of online data mining to improve your chances for victory.

TRACK YOUR RESULTS

This is important in any poker context, but especially crucial online where the hands come so fast and furious that your play tends to blur into an indeterminate fog. By tracking your results, you become responsible to yourself for what you do. You won't play monkeyfish poker, because you won't want to face the sad fact of that later. In other words, keep track of your results to keep yourself on track.

DON'T TRUST SHORT-TERM OUTCOMES

If you track your play and find that you're not turning the profit you thought you'd turn, remind yourself that your results may not be statistically valid yet. You have to book a lot of hours in any poker game before reliable trends emerge. If you lose your first five sessions, don't conclude you're a loser and quit. Likewise, if you win your first five sessions, don't imagine that you have the game licked. You've been inspired, or lucky, so far, but only hard work and concentration will keep your win rate high.

INVESTIGATE NEW SITES

Every new site that comes online comes with two opportunities. First, there's a promotional opportunity: They may be giving away free money, and you'll want to get your share. Second, more important, new sites attract new players with new money. Until they go broke, these new players with new money represent one of your most lucrative money-making opportunities online. Always keep an eye peeled for those new online rooms.

STRAIGHTFORWARD PLAY TAKES THE MONEY

Most online players lack sufficient discipline to play a sound, straightforward game of selective/aggressive Killer Poker. They call too much, which means that you'll make money by punishing them with your strong hands—*not* by bluffing. Only bluff when you're certain that no one else wants the pot. Otherwise just wait for strong hands and bet them as hard as you can.

WATCH BIG GAMES AND TOURNAMENTS

Even if you don't feel like investing a lot of money in online play, there are plenty of big games to sit in on and watch. Spend some time railbirding both big money games and big buy-in tournaments. Unlike the b&ms, you'll have an unobstructed view of every hand, and can give good, thoughtful study to which moves the players make and why. You can often learn more about poker by not playing poker at all.

AVOID PROMISCUOUS CALLING

Online players tend to call bets on the river quite promiscuously, a function of underestimating the unseen foe, no fear of facing shame for having made a dumb call, and just the general artificiality of the online environment. Try to bring your best real-world instincts to the online game: *If you know you're beat, don't call.* And the corollary to this: *If you know they'll call, don't bet.*

MULTITASK *MAYBE*

In most cases, players who divide their attention between online poker and anything else do themselves—and their bankrolls—a disservice. If, however, you have the specific problem of *indiscipline,* then giving yourself something to do between hands might keep you away from marginal calls, hopeless bluffs, and other reckless adventures.

PLAY TOURNAMENTS

Online tournaments offer a tremendous learning opportunity, because you get to see quite a lot of hands, quite a lot of "game" for a relatively small, and perfectly fixed, investment. As a bonus, much of what you learn about online tournament strategy is actually applicable to real-world tournaments, where picking off physical tells is less important than your overall game strategy. As a further bonus, *you might win!*

TEN "NEVERS"

1. Never play drunk
2. Never play tired
3. Never start a session you can't end on your own terms
4. Never show a hand you don't have to
5. Never use the pre-action buttons
6. Never let your chat betray your real skill level
7. Never play bigger than your bankroll allows
8. Never play against known superior foes

9. Never forget that the money is real
10. NEVER GAMBLE MORE THAN YOU CAN STAND
    TO LOSE

Now then, what tips of your own can you add to this trove?

_____

_____

_____

_____

_____

_____

_____

14

THE FUTURE OF ONLINE
POKER

"What's it going to be then, eh?" asks Alex, the nihilist pro-
tagonist of Anthony Burgess's sci-fi classic, *A Clockwork
Orange*. That novel depicts a future made bleak by lawless
teens, cowering citizens, and an ineffectual and uncaring
government. Written in 1962, the book paints vistas of social transformation, but anticipates very little in the way of
technological change: in the future of Burgess's imagination, people still write on *typewriters*.

It would have taken, of course, a seer of Nostradaman
stature to predict the whirlwind of technical (and therefore
social) revolution whipped up by the advent and popular-
ization of a single tool: the personal computer. Thanks to
this extraordinary desktop miracle, I can write this document, count the number of words in it, check the spelling
of "Nostradaman," verify the publication date of *A Clockwork Orange*, listen to music, monitor the progress of my favorite sports team, and of course play poker, all without
leaving the comfort of my home, office, or nearby Star-
bucks.

Concerning Internet poker, it's astounding to consider
how far the game has come in so little time. Hunting back

through the archives of rec.gambling.poker (something else I can do thanks to my dutiful PC), I find no reference to online poker sites as we know them before 1998. There were some free play sites online by then, and some (by today's standards) primitive precursors such as irc.poker. net and WRGPT, the World Rec.Gambling Poker Tournament, but the whole ball didn't really get rolling until 1999 and into the new millennium. Online poker, then, at least measured in historical terms, has existed for really only an eye blink.

The question is: How long will the eye blink last?

Will we all be looking back in 30 years (or even 20 or 10) and asking ourselves, "Whatever became of Internet poker?" Will the forces of repression have their way with the game and legislate it out of existence? Doubtful. In clashes between social engineers and technical engineers, the techies always win, and governments' or societies' efforts to stem the tide of technology amount to trying to stuff the genie back in the bottle.

In the 1980s, Japan had very stringent anti-pornography laws, and porn, for better or worse, was extremely hard to get. Then along came the fax machine and a subsequent storm of porn, furiously faxed among aficionados who could suddenly get all the prurient, albeit black-and-white, pictures they desired. Where are Japan's porn laws now?

Come to think of it, where is the fax machine now?

News item: September 2002,
Greece Bans All Video Games.

Comment: If Gameboys are outlawed,
only outlaws will have Gameboys.

The genie doesn't *go* back in the bottle. The genie *likes* being out.

Some social historians say that the death of the Soviet Union can be traced to the unstoppable wave of Western information and entertainment that broke over the Soviet Bloc in the late 1980s. How you gonna keep them down on the farm, so to say, after they've seen MTV?

Some social historians say that the death of the dark ages and the rise of the middle class in Europe in the fifteenth century can be traced to the advent of the printing press and a corresponding rise in literacy.

And probably some people didn't like that, and tried to stem the tide. (If moveable type is outlawed, only outlaws will have moveable type.) We can see how well that worked.

So now we look around this modern world of ours, and we see all sorts of objectionable (to some) activities taking place, thanks to the technological juggernaut of the Internet, which swarms across state and national boundaries, and mocks the laws of local jurisdictions.

When I was growing up, getting a copy of *Playboy* was a major coup. Now—*good God*—I delete ten spams a day that are more graphic than anything I could even have *imagined* as a kid. Some find it objectionable (I find it annoying), but no one can stop it, at least not now. Genie don't *want* to go home.

As an author, the last thing I want to see is the theft of my intellectual property, yet millions of people around the world casually engage in this act of theft every single day. Can you say MP3? Can you say CD burner?

Genie is cloned.

Genie is cloned.

Genie is cloned.

Internet gambling? A lot of people are dead opposed to

it. And they must feel pretty ineffectual right now. The credit card companies, we know, have taken a social or economic stand against it, as have the Greeks (that's what the whole banning video games thing was really all about, you know) and probably your local district attorney. Has Internet gambling gone away? Hah! Has porn?

Where does this leave Internet poker? Right out there on the same heaving sea of new technology as everything else. It will continue to grow and expand and develop and morph, and the law will be powerless to stop it. In all probability, if you wager real money on the Internet, you're breaking the laws of your home country, state, county, city or block. And they (whoever *they* are) can't do a damn thing about it. Not so long as there are countries like Costa Rica, Aruba, and the Federal Islamic Republic of the Comoros with a willingness to host site servers and laws (or lawlessness) that allow such things.

It's a big, strong genie now, spread loosely over the globe, and attacking it is exactly as effective as shoveling smoke.

Does this mean that you can expect to play Internet poker unimpeded into the sunny, bright tomorrow? Not necessarily.

Technology responds to other imperatives beyond the social and legal ones. Several prominent Internet poker sites have already gone belly-up. While it would seem like a license to print money (and yes, it's already being marketed as same), the fact is that running an online poker site is not a no-brainer. The site has to attract and hold the players, keep the game going, and hope that no revolution in the Federal Islamic Republic of the Comoros suddenly renders the server, well, ill-served.

So maybe, just maybe, Internet poker will go the way of the Betamax and the 5¼-inch floppy, leaving us back where we were: pursuing our buzz in the real world, trudging (or driving or flying) to the nearest cardroom we can find. But if that happens, if Internet poker vanishes from the face of your screen, it won't be for legal reasons.

How can I be so sure? After all, the best legal minds in the world are grappling with this question even as we speak. *They* don't know whether online poker is legal or not. It may be illegal in Arkadelphia, where you're playing, legal in Wagga Wagga, where your opponent sits, illegal in Great Britain, which your online cash transfer bank calls home, and yet again legal in Malagasy, site of the server. Which jurisdiction applies? And even if the sheriff of Arkadelphia decides that his word is law, what's he going to do? Bust down your door and take your computer? What about the guy's next door? That little old lady down the street? He can't bust everyone, even if he endows himself with the legal right to try.

So, again, if online poker is to die out soon, it will be for economic, not legal reasons.

Not that I see that happening. You can't swing a virtual dead cat these days without hitting a new poker site somewhere on the Internet. The promise of low start-up costs and low overhead is bringing new rooms online at a staggering rate. (Five new sites have launched since I started writing this book; one or two have probably launched since you started reading it.) At the same time, streams of new players are entering the game and building a base of people who find online poker a recreational option too good to pass up. This so-called second generation of online players has seen a number of big sites prove themselves with reliable servers, game security, and fast, hassle-free payouts, in a track record now stretching back some three or four years—an epoch in Internet terms. This generation has seen the suspected ogre of online collusion not turn out to be so daunting and dangerous as everyone once feared. They've discovered online tournaments, which give so much play for so little money. They have, in short, come to trust online poker as a convenient and safe place to feed their poker jones.

And I'm not sure how I feel about that. On one hand, I'm a responsible adult and I can control most aspects of my behavior, including the urge to play poker. On the other hand not everyone is, and not everyone can, and for them the lure of Internet poker is akin to the lure of a fisherman's worm: it may look like a snack, but really it's smack. Because it's so easy to get online and get into a game, certain at-risk personalities will definitely see their hobby turn into a habit and their habit into compulsion. I have no doubt that Internet poker will take its toll on the family finances, personal relationships, and self-esteem of a certain fixed percentage of the playing population. But so does real-world poker, and so do sports books and state lotteries and charity church bingo, so there you go.

See that sign on your computer? It says *Enter at Your Own Risk*.

See that other sign? It says *Handle with Care*.

I'm for freedom. I'm all in favor of freedom. If the city of Commerce, California, hadn't been free to license the Commerce Casino, I never would have discovered poker, and years of poker enjoyment, to say nothing of poker income, would have been absent from my life. So I'm for freedom—so for freedom, in fact, that I'm willing to endure porn spam or invitations to increase my manly girth or a zillion come-ons from online casinos, if that's the price I have to pay.

That's not a financial price, though, and as we contemplate the future of online poker, I would ask you to contemplate your own future in the context of the game. Will you make Internet poker another card in your well-rounded deck of recreations? Or will you make it the obsessive focus of your every waking hour? It has been said (and I think it's true) that you have to be at least a little obsessive to be a successful poker pro. But there's no law that says you have to be a poker pro. And certainly no law that says you'll succeed if you try. Why not be a successful poker amateur, someone who approaches the online game with seriousness, dedication, and a determination to win, but doesn't let it run his or her life?

Then the future will be bright indeed: for Internet poker, and for you.

Glossary

All-In Disconnect. A provision made by online sites to protect players who lose their Internet connection in the middle of a hand. A player who loses such connection is considered to be all-in for whatever bets he or she has made up to that point.

Avatar. A computer-generated character who represents you in an online game. Not all sites use avatars; some represent players with empty chairs or other icons.

b&m. Brick and mortar cardroom, a place to play live poker against live opponents whose faces you can actually see, as opposed to online cardrooms where you play live poker against live opponents whose faces you cannot see.

Bethole. When frenzied wagering and the dizzying pace of play combine to relieve a player of many chips quickly, he's said to be in an Internet bethole.

Book. A written record of your opponents' play in the past. Conscientious online players keep extensive book on their foes.

Bots. Short for robots. Poker playing software disguised as human foes.

Chat Box. A text window in which you can type messages to other players. Most sites offer you a *chat option*, which lets you select whether or not to read what the others have to say.

Chat Dork. Someone who chats not for strategic purposes but just to pass the time.

Chatterbox. A player who uses the text window as an aggressive tool for putting players on tilt through distracting, nonsensical, or confrontational chat.

Count Five Method. A strategy to prevent the time one takes to bet from being a tell. With the count five method, the player simply counts to five before taking all betting actions of any kind.

Cyberchips. Your online poker bankroll.

Double/Half Rule. A strategy for realizing real-world profit from online play, this rule suggests that every time players double through online, they take out half their profit as dividend. For example, if you parlay $500 into $1,000, you draw down $250 as profit.

Hand Log. A recorded history of the play of each hand. These can be downloaded directly from the site or sent to the player via e-mail upon request.

Hit-and-Run. A strategy for jumping into an online game, playing a few hands very aggressively, and jumping out before the other players know what hit them.

Hit-and-Run Bad. When that strategy fails.

Hundred-to-One Thumbnail. A rough means of calculating adequate bankroll for a given limit, whereby the bankroll equals one hundred times the big bet at that limit.

Mirplo. A momentary loss of consciousness that precipitates a strange, stupid, or counterproductive move in Internet poker. Named after an extraordinarily bad player of the same name.

Monkeyfish. A poker player who is both clueless and loose—commonly found online.

Monversation. One-way chat. When a player tries to goad, irk, or otherwise engage another player in online chat, but the other player refuses to rise to the bait, the first player is having a monversation.

Nonversation. No-way chat. When a player mutes another player's stream of chat, or disables his chat altogether, he's having a nonversation.

OMHS. One More Hand Syndrome. Because it's so easy to keep your online session going, it sometimes becomes hard to quit. If you find yourself saying "one more hand" or "one more round," you've got OMHS, and you need to see a doctor of discipline.

On Call. A player who's *on call* has ceased to care about card values and will play any hand he gets. Because most online players crave action above all, a high percentage of them are likely to be on call at any given time.

Onlineitis. A full-blown case of OMHS, in which the player not only can't leave the game, but can no longer even discern the urge to do so. Poverty is the natural result of—and sadly also the cure for—this disease.

Pre-Action Buttons. Clickable boxes that allow a player to decide in advance whether he or she wants to call, raise or fold, post blinds, or sit out.

Rake Surfing. Scouring online poker sites for the lowest possible rake at the limit you like to play.

Real World. Another name for the b&m environment.

Resource State. A poker player's most effective poker-playing state of mind. The speed with which you can enter an online game often means that your resource state lags well behind the fact of your presence in the game.

Suss Out. To learn or become familiar with the mechanics and functionality of an online site.

Waranoid. Wary to the point of paranoia. A common state

of mind for newcomers to online poker who over-invest in the fear that they're being colluded against or otherwise cheated online.

Wild chat. A style of online poker chat in which a player mixes truth and lies, sense and nonsense, signal and noise in an effort to obscure his or her true nature and skill level.

Winback. The irrational goal of a player on tilt and losing big. Playing quality poker no longer matters; his only concern is scoring a winback and climbing out of the hole he's dug for himself.

About the Author

JOHN VORHAUS has been playing poker since he could first clutch chips in his pudgy little hands, and he has been writing about the game since 1988. The only poker journalist to have written for *Card Player, Poker World,* and *Poker Digest,* he created the Killer Poker concept to codify his winning poker strategy of "Go big or go home." When not crushing the online game, John writes television and film scripts, and consults on film and TV projects worldwide. He lives in Monrovia, California, in the real world, and online at www.vorza.com.